Shadow Relationships

How to avoid them

Alfred Willowhawk

iii

Copyright © 2017 Alfred Willowhawk

ISBN10:1973802341

ISBN-13:978-1973802341

DEDICATION

This work is dedicated to my muse and partner
Willo' Wellspring.

CONTENTS

1 WHAT'S IN A NAME

The Shadow, it means many things to many people, and each person's interpretation of it is correct. This may seem a strange way to start a book that is focused on helping to illuminate our relationships from a shadow perspective, however, it is still true. The key thing to remember is that you created your shadow, as has every other person. No one has the inherent right to question or belittle anything that you have created for yourself.

C.J. Jung has much to say on the personal shadow. In his collected works he says, "the thing a person has no wish to be" [C.J. Jung, CW16, para 470]. This means that we place all that we do not like about ourselves in our shadow. This is a good thing, as that which we can place in the shadow we can take out of the shadow as well, it does not need to be an all or nothing kind of thing. Looking in another part of the Collected Works we see that Jung elaborates a bit by saying, "shadow is that hidden, repressed, for the most part inferior and guilt-laden personality whose ultimate ramifications reach back into the realm of our animal ancestor, [CW9 para 422], and in the next paragraph, " If it has been believed hitherto that the human shadow was the source of evil, it can now be ascertained on closer investigation that the unconscious man, that is his shadow does not consist only of morally reprehensible tendencies, but also displays a number of good qualities, such as normal instincts, appropriate reactions, realistic insights, creative impulses " [CW9 para 423].

So, what does happen to those "uncomfortable" or "unwanted" aspects of oneself? We place them in our shadow.

Those aspects of ourselves that we call "Shadow" are those aspects of our personality that we as individuals deem "not good". In order for us to say that something is not good, requires a judgment. A personal judgement that we make on ourselves due to a plethora of reasons. Some of these reasons are related to our social environment, our personal experience and other learned behaviors.. I have had many conversations with people who talk to me about how some individuals are DARK and others are LIGHT – what a crock. It is all energy. Energy just IS. The entire concept of Light being somehow innately GOOD and Dark being innately BAD is dreamed up by individuals and groups who wish to control large masses of people and take people's power away. Here is an example I really like.

A particular person grows up in a home where to be compassionate and sensitive is considered a "problem". As a child the compassion that the child showed was repressed, punished, etc. We are not talking about child rearing right now – so as an adult this person put compassion in their shadow – or – that place where we put things that we do not wish to present to the world!

A different person grows up in a home where to be angry and show it is a problem. As with the previous child signs of anger were repressed, punished, and as an adult this person is very quiet, does not show anger – they repress this aspect of themselves.

OK, NO JUDGEMENT here. BOTH of these examples are valid! So, repeat after me – there is no good, there is no bad, there is no good shadow and no bad shadow there is only ME!

Acceptance of all the aspects of oneself is one of the things that is important as one examines their own shadow. It is not easy, for sure.

People have whole lifetimes of what they "should" be. What they "could be". This is the coulda, shoulda, woulda syndrome and it is totally not useful. In the universe that I create for myself I know that them – I am human, and I know deep inside myself that I make mistakes, have a shadow and here is the key, I OWN that shadow, and take responsibility for it. The point is – the shadow is neither good nor bad it is part of the person and needs to be acknowledged and worked with. This is one of the purposes of Jungian psychology . In fact Jung said that unless we reach the point to recognize and integrate the shadow within it will continue to come out as repression or projection without conscious control of the individual. I do not know about you but for me – I am too much of a control freak to let any part of myself come out without control.

There is another aspect that Jung brings to the fore – and that is there is a collective Shadow that is prevalent and influences how one operates in the society at large. This is an interesting concept and for me it is yet another challenge that an individual works with to become the Best that it can be.

In some circles people say – Why does God let bad things happen to good people. Remembering that we said good and bad are judgments, but the point here is that people choose to do things from within. It means that the Divine does not cause a person to do anything. That statement above is what VICTIMS use to justify their own behaviors. If a person lives in an area where violence is the mode of operation for the bulk of their community – of course violence is going to be the primary mode of communication between them. It behooves us as individuals to "rise above" the circumstances and to CHOOSE a different path. SO, the answer to the question – Why does God or divine let bad things happen to good people is. The divine does not do it – people do it.

Here is another example from an old bumper sticker – Guns don't kill people - People kill people. I have yet to see a gun come automatically out of a holster or a waist band – jump into a person's hand and force the person to pull a trigger. The pulling of the trigger is an ACTION not a re-action. Think about that. Even the words tell us that there is something wonky with the thought process. There is ACTION and when we put the preface "R" "E" in front of it we are saying again. Yes, that is right the prefix "re" etymologically means again. So what we are saying when we say we are reacting to something is that we are acknowledging the action that was done and we are repeating it. I don't know about you but I don't play Simon Says and who the heck is Simon to tell me what to do anyway!

So we choose to place those things that do not serve us in our personal shadow and then the collective consciousness of the world we live in and the species we are part of has a shadow. This is where anomic or anti-normative behaviors come from.

This is part and parcel of who we all are, people. So, what do we have to fear of our own shadow? What truly is the Shadow's part in our own lives and how can we incorporate in a real and meaningful way the Shadow for ourselves and our relationships?

There is another aspect of the shadow that is related to our worldwide community Jung called it The Trickster, "…a collective shadow figure, a summation of all the inferior traits of character in individuals" [CW9 para 484]. The trickster is that part of our selves that is unconscious and unrelated, but someone who can nonetheless transform the meaningless into the meaningful. Often encountered at times of major decision points in our lives, the trickster is a moving target, that is showing things that we do not want to see, trying to show us the silliness of some of our own ideas through being the proverbial jester.

Looking at the shadow can be scary. All those aspects of ourselves that we bury deep down inside and hope to hide from ourselves that sometimes just break out when we least expect it. It is all a matter of perspective, sometimes the shadow can seem uncontrolled, and damaging to ourselves and others, yet at other times it is the more wild, "fun" seeking part of ourselves.

Both of these views of course are correct. It is all interpretation.. I am reminded of Iron John from Robert Bly in the Men's Mysteries work that I have done- we all have that part of ourselves that is difficult to get a handle on, and it does seem that we cannot control it.

Here is a secret – YOU ARE IN CONTROL! There are many ways that we learn how to put things in our shadow. And some of them are protective measures that we create due to experience with ourselves and the world around us. The aspect of ourselves that creates these measures is our emotions and our logic. Each time we have a trauma, especially emotional trauma we create a mechanism or measure to protect ourselves from being hurt again. We take the hurt itself and place it in our shadow. When we have a physical trauma our bodies convince us to not do that again and sometimes we place the situation that caused the physical hurt and put it in our shadow. Each of these things then gets "hidden" from our day to day walk until it either comes out on its own or we bring it out.

When a child of 3 or 4 stands in the kitchen and sees the hot stove they want to investigate. They reach for it to see the glowing fire or the bubbling pot or whatever. Usually a caregiver who sees this says something to try and stop the curious child from touching the hot item. In some cases the child still, still reaches and reaches until they get to see what they were trying to see – the hot pot. Well, we all know what happens, it BURNS and there is PAIN, in the most extreme case a child might file away touching the stove is painful and they do not want to ever touch it again – depending on the consequence of the action.

Now, in this hypothetical case the child never goes to the stove again, and over time places so much of the " I am not touching a stove again" into their awareness that as an adult they still will not use a stove.

The original issue was way long ago, yet the compensatory mechanism is not to go near a stove. Over time they have forgotten what occurred, and yet they still will not use a stove. As an adult they use a Microwave but the stove in their brand new apartment is always clean. They do not know why they do not like stoves but they do not like them. Sitting deep in their shadow is the hurt, (physical) from when they touched the stove and got burned really badly. They decide that they are going to work through the issue, and then the emotions get involved and they lash out in anger at anyone who is trying to "convince them" that the stove is ok. Its irrational but it just comes out. This is what the shadow in this case does. It uses tools that are in it to protect the person.

As we do more shadow work with ourselves it's about accommodation and understanding. Three little words – Knowledge, Wisdom and Understanding. It's not easy to move ourselves toward a better understanding, it's about taking control of ourselves. Yet even that control is by consensus of everything in our personal and societal world.

See yourself sitting in the room objectively observing the shadow and non-shadow sitting in chairs. What does your shadow look like? It's not scary, it's just you. Remember that our logical minds can deceive us too. I remember one individual whose emotional shadow self was dark, with fangs, and claws and big yellow eyes. Another person's shadow was obese, sloppy and they even smelled them – it was not pretty. In another case the shadow was a professor with glasses, perfectly dressed as an Edwardian Era Peer.

Each of us puts together what we see based on the inner workings of ourselves. These pictures are the clues we use to begin our integration of our shadow. Here is a good method to begin this process.

The first step in any relationship is to meet and acknowledge your shadow. Yes, that's right meet it and acknowledge its existence. It's a relationship- not a battle – a relationship, use your favorite vision. For me I would imagine a coffee shop where I am sitting by the fire, in a wingback chair, reading a book with my favorite coffee drink – Expresso Americano – no accounting for taste there – reading the same book as me, but the words are backwards. I can see the cover and it's the same book yet the words are right to left instead of left to right. I look over the top of my book and see that the person is also looking up at me. I start a conversation, say Hi, introduce myself and go back to reading. The person acknowledges my Hi and introduces themselves imagine that their name is derfla. Alfred spelled backwards. We both go back to reading our books. The next day we are in the coffee shop again together, and this time we start a conversation.

It's important to BUILD a relationship with your Shadow, start SMALL. Start with one aspect of yourself and let the relationship between that body and its shadow start a relationship. After a while sharing thoughts, aspirations, opinions – THIS is beginnings of integration and accommodation between the shadow and the non-shadow. To not use the words Light and Dark or Shadow and Light, prevent judgment and call them shadow and non-shadow, or just call it the self.

Work on this, no fear, no pain, no past, no future only now and integration. It will take time and some of the work might be uncomfortable, however, in the end you will see when the completely integrated shadow are with you the strength of the energy we send to the center of ourselves and you will be unstoppable and will manifest your truest desires!

If one thinks about the changes in the seasons, after the middle of summer the nights become longer and the days become shorter. There is not much apparent time to complete all the tasks of the day. For some they wake up when its dark, go about their day, and come home in the dark. It's almost as if there is no day. No light. This is what it sometimes feels like when the shadow is manifesting. It breeds discontent, depression, and anxiety. Looking and hearing what is deep in our own shadows helps us to heal and become stronger more complete individuals. It does not matter how old you are chronologically, or even how old you are emotionally. What matters is how we assimilate and accommodate information. I am sharing a paradigm that you may or may not have thought about. I encourage you to look at this from a new perspective.

Can you work to build that relationship with the deepest parts of yourself.

The way to do this is to release judgment on yourself and others. Release it so that you can learn from each new experience and take responsibility for your actions and let others take responsibility for theirs!

No one controls you, YOU are the controller! Its ok to let go of societies strictures on your being. Societies expectations are not your expectations. Commune with the world around you in the way that you desire. It does not matter what your shadow says about your body, it's your body, accept it!

This is just one example this is one of the things that our North American Society imposes on us through telling us what the perfect body is, what the perfect clothes are, all of this is seeking to control our world and what we do in it. Find your own special place that you can release whatever you and your shadow decide to share and ENJOY it!

2 BUILDING RELATIONSHIP WITHIN

Last chapter was about the shadow within ourselves and how some of what we place there is what we accept as societal control. We also said that all of us want to take back or enhance our control of ourselves without allowing anyone else to control us.

We also talked about building a relationship with our shadow selves just as we build relationship with the non-shadow self.

Myth can be seen as a way to tap into things that are uncomfortable. A way to objectively analyze what is going on within oneself and the world around them. There is one myth of Celtic origin called, We are The Dueling Brothers – The Holly King and the Oak King.

This myth is also related to the changing of the seasons, the growing and lessening of the light and warmth of the sun, the changes from Spring through Winter. There are two main energies that are represented by these two brothers. They are personified as the energy of fertility, growth, death, and rebirth. In the myth there are two faces – The Holly King and the Oak King. These are the two "opposing" energies of the moving of the year from Spring to Summer, from Summer to Autumn, and from Autumn to Winter..

On one level each of the twin energies rule for half of a year, and then dies. But the defeated twin is not truly dead, he merely withdraws for six months. One more point the year itself is divided into a dark and light half. The Light half of the year starts at Midwinter and ends at Midsummer. The Dark Half of the year begins at Midsummer and ends at Midwinter. The Oak King, rules from midwinter to midsummer. The Holly King rules the dark half of the year from Midsummer to Midwinter.

Ok, so we have stated that light and dark are words not judgments and we ended last chapter with a challenge to meet and begin a relationship with our Shadow selves. As I encouraged last chapter, no judgment of ourselves, we certainly do not say that the dark half of the year is "bad" and the light half is "good". It is only a way of differentiating these two sides of the same coin. In fact we know that astronomically that the orbital mechanics of the earth is part of the reason why there is this cycle of longer nights during the dark half of the year and longer days during the light half of the year.

If we go beyond the myth and the astronomical mechanics we can look at these as Archetypes then we can really learn a few things to help us with our Shadow and Nonshadow selves.

The Holly king rules during the dark times. Imagine that the holly king is the shadow of the Oak King and the Oak king is the Shadow of the Holly king. What might this look like?

There is no specific source myth, however, descriptions of the Holly King are interpretive and tend to vary. In one tradition he is described as an immortal giant wielding a large club of holly wood. He is "the lord of darkness, death, animals and withering … a horned god … the avenger, older, whose wild hunt runs free to protect and avenge". Others interpret the Holly King as more jovial, and potentially as an early precursor to Santa Claus. Traditional British Christmas carol "The Holly and the Ivy" makes reference to the Holly King, saying: *Of all the trees that are in the wood The holly wears the crown.*

The Holly King aids individuals in workings for material gain, physical revenge, beauty, protection ,luck and dream magic. He is the guardian of the way to the Goddess for death and rebirth. He is also associated with Fire and household protection.

Let's look a little deeper though. The Holly king DOES have thorns after all. Ever see a Holly bush? How about those red berries what are THEY representing.

One of the aspects of the Holly King that is shadow like is his propensity for physical revenge. Physical revenge is not necessarily a negative attribute, after all, we CAN protect ourselves, but if unchecked by logic the emotional component of revenge can really let loose. I think of some of the myths around dragons who are disturbed that burn whole villages instead of the one person who bugged them. Fire, can burn to heat but also become a raging torrent that destroys everything it touches.

Other more negative characteristics can be found by looking at the zodiac for some of the signs within the Holly King's reign. Let's just look at one of these – Sagittarius. Careless, impatient, tactless are the more negative aspects of Sagittarius.

They are prone to taking things for granted, and taking unnecessary risks. Tactless, their honesty can sometimes be too brutal, which hurts others, impatient they can be restless and can push things too far. Inconsistent Their interest in things can be short-lived, and keeps fluctuating. Thus they end up being less efficient than they can be. They find it extremely difficult to deliver consistent performance. Now, remember we are not judging here only looking at these things to see how and if the Holly King and the Oak King are shadows for each other.

To give fair review, let's look at the Oak King. The Oak King aids individuals in healing, material gain, longevity, strength, connection to the divine. SO there are some similarities between the twins. Material gain certainly stands out as one of those things. Notice however that where the Holly King has connection to physical revenge the Oak King fosters connection to the divine. This to me is the most glaring aspects that show a clear "Yin and Yang" or Shadow and Non Shadow between the brothers. So, like the Holly King when we looked at Sagittarius let us look at one of the zodiac signs of the Oak King or Light Half of the year.

To make our example easy I chose the opposite or astrologically complimentary sign of Gemini. Gemini is the mutable air sign of the zodiac. Gemini's are very adept at intellectualizing through communication. So a Gemini is always willing to hear a different paradigm to their own viewpoints. Their negative characteristics are failure to focus either energy or intellect. They speak their mind regardless of the consequences and do not like staying in one place as they feel this is stagnation. They also can be very superficial in their examination of things rather than taking the time to truly analyze what is going on. Gemini and Sagittarius are concerned with communication, information and knowledge. Both signs are curious truth-seekers who receive and organize their world differently. To give a truly integrated look before we look at the shadowing aspect of both the Holly and the Oak King more deeply let's take a couple of minutes to look at how two perspective individuals who are Gemini and Sagittarius work together as an example of HOW the Shadow and Non Shadow of individuals can create a really awesome whole! I particularly like the way that it is put together in Ada Aubin and June Rifkins book **The Complete Book of Astrology** from 1988 and Joanna Martin Woolfolk, **The Only Astrology Book You'll Ever Need.** 2006 From these two books we get that

The Sagittarius partner will be inspired by the ideas of the Gemini to use his own creativity. Juices .In one sense Gemini fans Sagittarius' fir. As Gemini is also a master of details and facts this helps Sagittarius put her "big picture" into action.

The Gemini is entertained by Sagittarius' charm and quick wit. Gemini likes colorful individuals and he finds this in a Sagittarius. From Sagittarius, a Gemini can learn to take a more optimistic view of things. They will also be encouraged to be more spontaneous. Geminis have a tendency to keep things bottled up, which a clever and utterly frank Sagittarius can usually get out of them. A Gemini can also gain a sense of the bigger picture and become more adventurous hence together they are amazing philosophers!

Notice a few things here? IF we look closely we see that the ability of the Sagittarius to focus (a non-shadow characteristic) helps the Gemini's apparent inability to focus. This is how two individuals can work together by becoming each other's balance.

So the Holly King proverbially has in his shadow the inability to focus, risk taking, tactless, and a seeker of revenge and the Oak King's shadow proverbially has in his shadow under analysis, a people pleaser, and always giving in too much.

See how the two are examples? When we spoke just a minute ago about how these two individuals Sagittarius and Gemini can complement each other how do we come to the place where our own twins can complement each other? It is a truly awesome experience to be able to have your shadow and non-shadow take over each other This truly creates a Beautiful soul.

As we look at ourselves it is the same thing. The Oak and Holly King though they fight occasionally do work together. If you remember from last week we decided that the shadow was a place where those aspects of ourselves reside and unless we come to an accommodation with it – it will come out uncontrolled. So let's look at the mechanism for integrating shadow. We finished off last chapter by encouraging ourselves to start relationship building with our shadows.

The emotional shadow and nonshadow are a good place to start. I look to mythology to help us get over any hurdle that says I am talking about a person I know, even myself!

In the Mabinogion the Welsh compendium of myth in the second branch there are two seemingly side characters. Nyssim and Evnyssim. They are brothers and cousins of Bran and Branwen. Nyssim is steady, quiet, and intellectual while Evnyssim is boisterous, quick to anger and a do-er not a thinker. In the Myth Bran and Branwen choose to align themselves with the Eyrie people (thats Ireland by the way), after consensus building with the other princes, both male and female, of Wales. Nyssim was at the conclave and voted for the association and Branwen consented to become the Queen of Eyrie. She consented after meeting and spending time with the King of Eyrie by the way she was absolutely part of the discussions and there is a line in the Mabinogia that shows that if she would not have consented then the deal would be off. SO, she was a MAJOR part of the discussions and the decision.

OK, so in comes Evnyssim and he is told of the decision and he is HOT, Really Angry and goes out and defaces all the horses of the Erye. As the Irish look at horses as the representative of the Goddess and their anointing as kings they are justifiably upset and call the whole deal off. Bran for his part apologizes or Evnyssim and as High King takes the responsibility for his actions and gifts the Irish with a series of things that we do not have time to go through and each of these things have significance as well. What is important for our discussions is the difference in the behavior of Evnyssim and Nyssim. IF we look at the characteristics in a grid we see the following.

Where Nyssim was steady Evnyssim was quick. Where Nyssim was calculating in his responses Evnyssim was prone to action. Where Nyssim was calm Evnyssim was boisterous and quick to anger.

It is my belief, and I personally have not found any research from scholars to back this up, that Nyssim and Evnyssim may be the twins like the Oak and Holly King, or representative of non-shadow and shadow.

What characteristics of ourselves do we hold in the shadow? If we try to be unemotional in our responses to the world then we hold fast emotion in our shadow. If we are not very intellectual we hold our intellectual potential in our shadow. I am sure that you can come up with many more examples within yourself.

The next step is to allow that all aspects of ourselves are OK. No judgment here remember? We choose what we allow the world to see and what we deal with in our own reality.

I once was listening to the Holiday Message from Krishna Das and he related a story that shows this really well. He said that there was a weekend retreat that was about lovingkindness. In this retreat the first day the participants said a couple of mudras over and over again. One of them was I am Happy and another was I am healthy. He said that after a few hours of this people are just saying th words over and over. No meaning behind them. The next day the participants were told to think of a person that has always been there for them and to say YOU are Happy and YOU are Healthy. Amazingly enough the participants really felt something then. After that they were told to go back to saying those things about themselves and some remembered and felt the Divine within but others did not.

This is indicative of or relationship with our shadows. We need to cultivate an acceptance of those aspects of ourselves that we do not like. There is nothing inside me that is not useful and entitled to love by me. This is the key. Yes, you can be whole. It's OK if there are aspects of yourself that to the world are not so good. It's all in the presentation! Kind of like a meal at a really good restaurant vs a fast food restaurant. The same hamburger, fries and drink presented on a plate, with some garnish and a well toasted open faced bun seems to be better in some people's minds than the same hamburger and fries in a paper sack wrapped in paper and a drink in a paper cup!

Our shadow can be like that fast food item or like the restaurant item. My encouragement for this week is to pick one aspect of yourself. Then write down all the positive things about that aspect. Then write down the negative characteristics of that same aspect. BE honest with yourself!

Here is an example to help you along.

Let's call this person Paul

Paul decides to look at his emotions both shadow aspects and non-shadow aspects.

Positive Emotional Characteristics

- Cares for Animals

- Accepts other people's feelings as genuine

- Judges no one

- Is demonstrative in appropriate ways to those he is in relationship with

- a good listener

-

Negative Emotional Characteristics that are in his Shadow

- A short fuse

- Judgment of every action taken by him and around him

- Knowledge of his superiority over most people

- Wanting to be coddled and taken care of by others

Ok, so these are really easy to see as opposites and in most of us the lines are more grey than black and white but you get the idea.

Next step

Paul writes down instances where he learned some of those behaviors. In other words, for the shadow when did he first notice that he had a short fuse. When was the first time it "came out" what was the situation. He does that for both the shadow and the non-shadow.

In general Paul seems to the outside world to be very accommodating. He does not ever seem to take a stand on anything, and always goes with the flow. One day he flies off the handle at someone and starts to only do things that THEY want to do, not caring at all about anyone else or the consequences of the actions they are taking. This is the example of the Shadow taking over for a time. I can imagine the emotional shadow stewing and stewing and finally losing it and just coming out.

A different paradigm is as follows:

Paul feels uncomfortable with a particular issue going on, and gathers up the power of the shadow's ability to utilize his knowledge of the situation and speak it in a kind and gentle way but holding his ground. See, integrating what is in the emotional shadow and bringing it out in a balanced and harmonious world.

This is what we have to look forward to, it's a lot of work, but it can be done. This is part of the personal integration work between our shadow and non-shadow consciousness. And it is from here that we begin to realize that we are able to do and be so much more than what is perceived by the general population. Once an individual becomes aware of what is going on in their own minds, they can begin to mitigate those things that disturb them, and find new ways to act. It begins the process of living within a vibrational pattern that is one of balance and harmony. As we expand our mind to be conscious of our unconscious mind, we can experience more and more of these qualities while in our physical form.

Indigos carry this awareness, which is the key to multi-dimensionality, and it leads them to be warriors for causes that heal the Earth. Realization and practice that no one is greater than the other and that group consciousness is the path to the future. We must all cooperate for the good of all to create a better Earth.

Once one becomes aware of where they are, and what they are doing they can begin to live in Unconditional Love, Unconditional Forgiveness, and Unconditional Acceptance. We hold no judgement, guilt, or negativity towards ourselves and strive to remember we live in harmony with ourselves. At this level, we are free to create new ways of thinking/being/doing through the seeds of unity consciousness.

3 I HAVE NEEDS

Every person has needs. Some of them we store in our shadow. This is because many of us have been taught by parents, family, friends, and society that these needs are either not necessary or selfish. The truth is, to some extent we are all selfish. Remember that in this entire book, we keep saying no judgment. There is no one that is completely selfless. It is true that there are varying levels of selfness, however, there is always a part of the self that wants its needs met. In this chapter we are going to examine one system called the Hierarchy of Human Needs. This hierarchy helps us to understand the why of the things we do, say, accept and frankly do not accept within our personal universes.

Abraham Maslow (1954) posited this hierarchy of human needs based on two groupings: deficiency needs and growth needs. Within the deficiency needs, each lower need must be met before moving to the next higher level. Once each of these needs has been satisfied, if at some future time a deficiency is detected, the individual will act to remove the deficiency. The first four levels are:

1) Physiological: hunger, thirst, bodily comforts, etc.;

2) Safety/security: out of danger;

3) Belongingness and Love: affiliate with others, be accepted; and

4) Esteem: to achieve, be competent, gain approval and recognition.

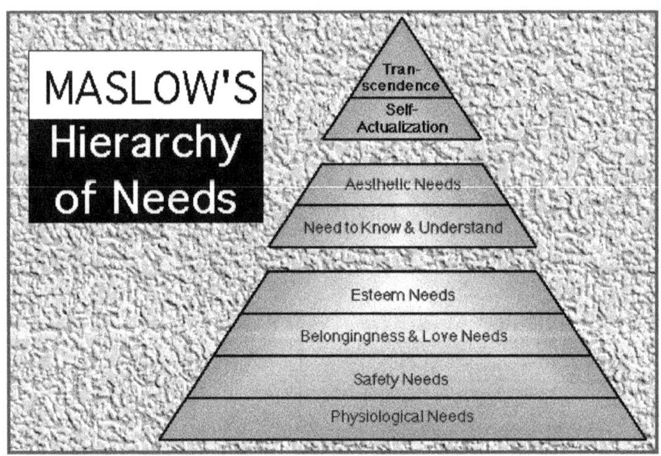

According to Maslow, an individual is ready to act upon the growth needs if and only if the deficiency needs are met. The ultimate goal is to become a self-actualized individual. As we become more in tune with our own shadow, reach accommodation with them, lose judgment of self and others we become more self-actualized. Self-actualized people are characterized by individuals who have accomplished and incorporated the following 6 processes.

1) being problem-focused

2) incorporating an ongoing freshness of appreciation of life

3) a concern about personal growth

4) the ability to have peak experiences.,

5) Cognitive: to know, to understand, and explore

6) Aesthetic: symmetry, order, and beauty

Once an individual reaches this level of the pyramidical structure then they tap

7) Self-actualization: to find self-fulfillment and realize one's potential

8) Self-transcendence: to connect to something beyond the ego or to help others find self-fulfillment and realize their potential.

Maslow's basic position is that as one becomes more self-actualized and self-transcendent, one becomes more wise (develops wisdom) and automatically knows what to do in a wide variety of situations. Daniels (2001) suggested that Maslow's ultimate conclusion that the highest levels of self-actualization are transcendent in their nature may be one of his most important contributions to the study of human behavior and motivation.

Norwood (1999) proposed that Maslow's hierarchy can be used to describe the kinds of information individual's seek at different levels of development. For example, individuals at the lowest level seek **coping information** in order to meet their basic needs. Information that is not directly connected to helping a person meet his or her needs in a very short time span is simply left unattended. Individuals at the safety level need **helping information**. They seek to be assisted in seeing how they can be safe and secure. **Enlightening information** is sought by individuals seeking to meet their belongingness needs. Quite often this can be found in books or other materials on relationship development. **Empowering information** is sought by people at the esteem level. They are looking for information on how their egos can be developed. Finally, people in the growth levels of cognitive, aesthetic, and self-actualization seek **edifying information**. While Norwood does not specifically address the level of transcendence, I believe it is safe to say that individuals at this stage would seek information on how to connect to something beyond themselves or to how others could be edified.

See how these are utilized? Ok, so as is usually the case this has evolved over the years especially since this was first proposed by Maslow over 50 years ago.

Remember here we are talking about motivation. So within the context of understanding our shadow this is part of the fuel that drives us as individuals to improve, and interact with ourselves and the others as well as our society

What has come about over the years is that there are three levels of human needs. IT has been massaged and proposed Gordon Allport (1960, 1961) who incorporated concepts from systems theory into his work on personality.

Alderfer's Hierarchy of Motivational Needs

Level of Need	Definition	Properties
Growth	Impel a person to make creative or productive effects on himself and his environment	Satisfied through using capabilities in engaging problems; creates a greater sense of wholeness and fullness as a human being
Relatedness	Involve relationships with significant others	Satisfied by mutually sharing thoughts and feelings; acceptance, confirmation, under- standing, and influence are elements

Existence	Includes all of the various forms of material and psychological desires	When divided among people one person's gain is another's loss if resources are limited

Maslow recognized that not all personalities followed his proposed hierarchy. While a variety of personality dimensions might be considered as related to motivational needs, one of the most often cited is that of introversion and extroversion. Reorganizing Maslow's hierarchy based on the work of Alderfer and considering the introversion/extraversion dimension of personality results in three levels, each with an introverted and extroverted component. This organization suggests there may be two aspects of each level that differentiate how people relate to each set of needs with different personalities relating more to one dimension than the other. For example, an introvert at the level of Other/Relatedness might be more concerned with his or her own perceptions of being included in a group, whereas an extrovert at that same level would pay more attention to how others value that membership.

A Reorganization of Maslow's and Alderfer's Hierarchies

Level	Introversion	Extroversion
Growth	Self-Actualization (development of competencies [knowledge, attitudes, and skills] andcharacter)	Transcendence (assisting in the development of others' competencies and character;relationships to the unknown, unknowable)
Other (Relatedness)	Personal identification with group, significant others (Belongingness)	Value of person by group (Esteem)
Self (Existence)	Physiological, biological (including basic emotional needs)	Connectedness, security

If we take this and apply it to our discussion we see some interesting correlations. The Growth level – self-actualization is where depending on our introversion and extroversion personality gives us different results. It is why we take both into account in our conversations as we reach consensus within ourselves for ourselves. As we become more self-actualized, or in consensus with our own shadow we are focusing our energies on assisting in the development or facilitating other people's growth. This is how we fuel our own desires to manifest the reality we truly desire and avoid toxic relationships with ourselves and others.

SO, depending upon our personality type in terms of introversion or extroversion it may be harder or easier for us to connect and grow within ourselves and the universe both within and without. Here is an interesting fact, we all have both introversion and extroversion within ourselves. Some of it is in our shadow, other parts not.

Yes, you heard me. Each of us has both introversion and extroversion inside us. Introversion is a type of receptive energy and extroversion is a kind of projective energy. I utilize a tool with new students called the KTS II which is a psychological test that is based on the MBTI personality test. This test or Temperament sorter helps an individual to see their non-shadow and shadow scale and really gives one the ability to tap into both aspects of themselves.

As we incorporate more of the lessons that we have learned, accepting those consequences for our own actions, and re-assessing our own behavior we reach higher and higher levels of consciousness.

IT is at these higher levels of consciousness that pettiness, jealousies, lying, and other generally anomic behaviors disappear. I see people who use justify to themselves on a daily basis to prove that they can manipulate others to their own way of doing things.

To justify their own behaviors on the imagined slights that others have "caused" on them. Words like – He or she made me do it, or That person is a bad person so I need to make sure that they do not hurt others by spreading gossip and telling the world all about them.

These behaviors have no place in the balanced individual. I for one choose not to waste my energy on individuals who are justifying their choices that deliberately cause harm to another. I am not saying that I "turn the other cheek", I am more of a give them enough rope and they will hang themselves kind of guy.

See this is the choice I make, not to waste energy on what I perceive to be wasteful things. In this I have created a defense that I use as a filter in all my relationships. These defenses are like any other kind of defense. Think about a wall. A wall around a property does two things right? You all have heard this before, it keeps stuff out but it also keeps stuff in.

Now here is a secret to our inner defenses. They are not helpful. I do not mean that we should not defend ourselves. That is silly, and a balanced individual always is defending themselves to some degree. What I mean here is that when our defenses are so strong that they change the information that comes through our filters to be attacking us, even when they are not attacking us, it becomes a problem.

Have you heard the saying – keep your friends close and your enemies closer? What this means is that those we choose to perceive as enemies, are only enemies because of the choices they make. I do NOT choose to have enemies. I choose to look at those individuals who seek to ride my coat tails, another old saying, plant seeds of discord yet never "cross the line" to actually talk about a person, who justify their own lack of self-worth, by projecting those feelings on another, and a myriad of other behaviors that are just plain sad, to have compassion for them, and even bring them close to be watched, and certainly protect myself to the extent of here I the key – doing what I always do! I do not change my actions, opinions, or deeds based upon any other persons interpretation of events. I make my own decisions how? By allowing myself to question my own interpretations of every action BEFORE I take that action.

This is relatedness and growth as we discussed before. As individuals it is important to stay in the balance between introversion and extroversion, using the information above and accept BOTH aspects of ourselves. Balance and Harmony once again!

4 FLUIDITY OF SHADOW

SO here is the proposition - the non-shadow and Shadow, are fluid. That what is shadow for the shadow is the non-shadow and vis a versa SO we can begin to see the "grey" aspect of reality. This is important as there are truly no absolutes. There is only grey, nothing is black and white only.

Let's look at some of the shadow aspects of the individual that are not detrimental to the non-shadow and also are the non-shadow aspects of the Shadow.

We said in a previous chapter that that the Shadow of a person according to Jungian Psychology held not only those things we do not like about ourselves but some things that are useful to us at certain times.

I like to look at these things as a cabinet with many shelves that hold those things that are currently not useful to me but MAY be useful to me at certain times. For me, one of those things is what I call my intransience. When I was working to truly have the tools to continuingly integrate my shadow and non-shadow myself one of the things that my mentors said to me was that I was hyper focused on things when I was working on them and would move toward the goal regardless of what was going on around me. So, as time went on I learned that this was not something that was good for the goal, me, or my relationships.

What I put in shadow was my determination to succeed. This then is one of those things for me that is useful sometimes but not so useful other times.

OK, so I pull this out when I intuit that it is necessary and then look to taper it or modify it with other aspects decision making or choices. For me I use consensus building to mitigate that hyper focus.

The ability to focus on a task or goal in and of itself is a good thing, but when it becomes totally me centered it's not so good. So, not divesting myself of this part of myself but mitigating the negative aspects of it with consensus building is a way to prevent myself from disturbing the balance of myself and others and still accomplishing the goal or task.

OK, so ONE framework for our shadow self is our Ego. We know from Psychology that it is important to HAVE and Ego, in fact we all do, it's when it becomes overpowering it becomes Egotistical and negative.

What is the Ego? Carl Jung described and divided the psyche into three parts the Ego, the Personal Unconscious, and the Collective Unconscious.

The Ego is additionally known as the self by Jung, according to (Jung, 1965) in (Maltby, Day, & Macaskill, 2010) as humans the ego is responsible for our feelings of identity. (Maltby, Day, & Macaskill, 2010) The ego holds memories from prior experiences relating to the thoughts and feelings in regards to individuals behaviors. The ego is quite akin to Freud's meaning and has sense of self. Personal identity or ego developed around the age of four according to Jung (Friedman& Shustask, 2006).

In his work The Undiscovered Self he says: *Anyone who has any ego-consciousness at all takes it for granted that he knows himself. But the ego knows only its own contents, not the unconscious and its contents. People measure their self-knowledge by what the average person in their social environment knows of himself, but not by the real psychic facts which are for the most part hidden from them. In this respect the psyche behaves like the body, of whose physiological and anatomical structure the average person knows very little too. ["The Undiscovered Self," CW*

10, par. 491.]

There are four ways of interpreting reality are the four ego-functions - Sensation, Thinking, Feeling, and Intuition. These consist of two diametrically-opposed pairs. Thinking is the opposite of Feeling, and Sensation the opposite of Intuition. So, suggests Jung, if a person has the Thinking function (an analytical, "head"-type way of looking at the world) highly developed, the Feeling function (the empathetic, value-based "heart"-type way of looking at things) will be correspondingly undeveloped, and in fact suppressed. The same goes for Sensation and Intuition. Sensation is orientation "outward" to physical reality, and Intuition "inward" to psychic reality.

Jung perceived of these four Ego-functions as making up a kind of scale. The upper part of the scale is shown light, meaning that it is the developed conscious faculty, and the other part dark, meaning that it is the undeveloped or suppressed unconscious faculty. (Indeed, much of Jung's work involved recognition of the dichotomy of Light and Dark, Conscious and Unconscious). The faculty which is most Conscious (in this case "Thinking") is the dominant one, or Principal function, and the other one ("Intuition") is the secondary faculty, or Auxiliary function. So we have one function in full consciousness and fully developed, another function as secondary to this, a third function, the opposite of the second, as slightly suppressed and unconscious, and the fourth, the opposite of the first, as totally unconscious.

Ok, so in laymen's terms what this is saying is that the ego is complex and is part of what allows everyone to flow between shadow and non-shadow. HA! A HUGE purpose for our Ego.

The four Ego-Functions by the way as you see above create two pairs. I propose that we look at each of the individual items of the pairs as one aspect of the continuum between the non-shadow and the Shadow. Ok, let me be specific!

The first pair is Thinking and Feeling.

The logic or Thinking is in the LIGHT and the Feeling is in the Shadow. The second pair is Sensation in the light and Intuition in the Shadow.

THINKING refers to the faculty of rational analysis; of understanding and responding to things through the intellect, the "head" so to speak. Thinking means connecting ideas in order to arrive at a general understanding. The Thinking-type often appears detached and unemotional. The Scientist and the Philosopher are examples of the "thinking type".

FEELING is the interpretation of things at a value- level, a "heart"-level rather than a "head"-level.   Feeling evaluates, it accepts or rejects an idea on the basis of whether it is pleasant or unpleasant. According to Jung this is the emotional personality type.

SENSATION means conscious perception through the sense-organs. The Sensation personality-type relates to physical stimuli. But there is a difference according to whether the person is an introvert or an extrovert.

Finally, INTUITION is like sensation in that it is an experience which is immediately given to consciousness rather than arising through mental activity (e.g. thinking or feeling). But it differs in that it has no physical cause. It constitutes an intuition or hunch, a "gut"-level feeling, or an "ESP" experience. It is the source of inspiration, creativity, and novel ideas. According to Jung, the Intuitive type jumps from image, is interested in a while, but soon loses interest.

Thinking and Feeling are both rational, in that they both require an act of Judgment. Sensation and Intuition are both irrational, in that they involve no reason, but simply result from stimuli (whether external or internal) acting upon the individual.

Ok, so if an individual only operates in the logical or thinking place then they can be perceived as cold, calculating etc. Oppositely a person who only operates from feeling can be perceived as over emotional, over empathetic.

So first a couple of things about those who are Sensation type individuals. So, we could have an Introverted-Sensation type, such as an artist, who experiences the physical world (sensation) from the perspective of the psychic or inner consciousness (introversion). As opposed to this, the Extroverted-Sensation type would be the person who is a simple materialist or hedonist, interested only in physical or pragmatic things. This type tends to be realistic and practical. At worst, one may be crudely sensual.

Now with these two if an individual is basically focused on only their intuition then they can be perceived as air headed, or non-committal since they are waiting for answers or only accepting the answers that come to them without any assistance. The opposite of this is one who is only accepting of what they see and can sometimes become hedonistic.

However, if we look at these in terms of shadow and non-shadow we see that BOTH aspects work together.

The picture on the next page, (figure 1) is the "Shadow Mandala". It is a tool to assist in understanding the inner workings of the shadow within an individual. There is also a non-shadow mandala (figure 2) that can be utilized in the same way as the shadow mandala. The <u>Warrior Within Release Program,</u> is a program I have developed that defines the **Spiritual Warrior,** and gives an individual the tools to integrate and utilize both the shadow and non-shadow in creating a balanced and harmonious life for each person. This program is also part of *The Warrior Within Show* on WCAS-DB, (<u>http://thecauldron.net</u>) all of which can be accessed at <u>http://thewarriorwithinrelease.com</u>.

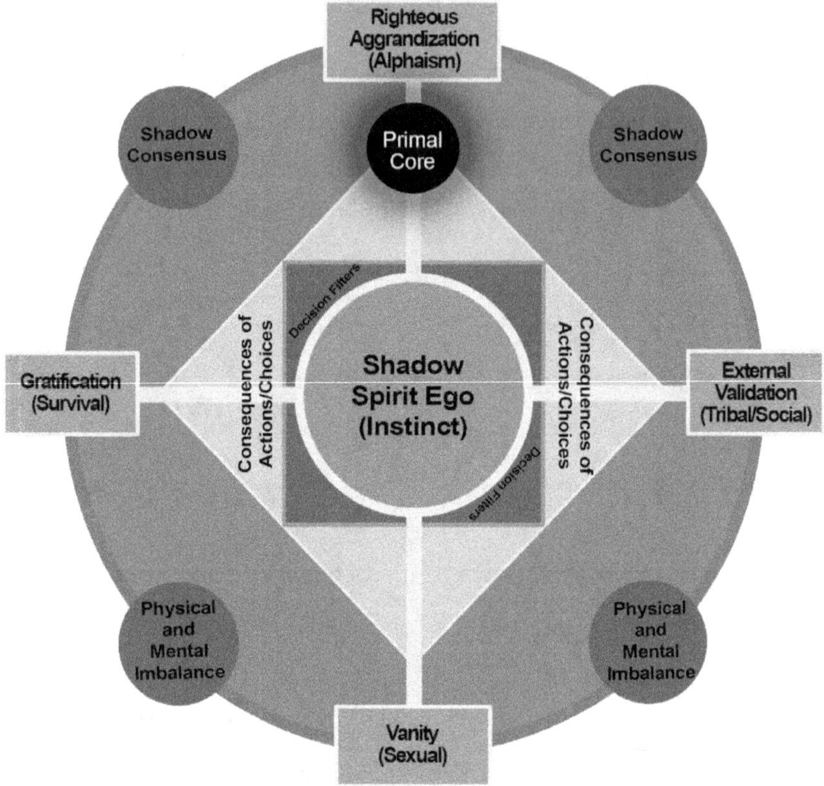

Figure 1

Let's look at one aspect of the shadow mandala and then show how these conduits work. There are four "aspects" of the shadow in the cardinal north, south, east and west. The four major aspects are Vanity, Alphaism, External Validation and Gratification.

These four aspects of Ego – act as information gatherers and conduits to the Instinct or That which we do without thinking.

We can call this the Ego as well and is the INSIDE or the

BALANCE of the non-shadow mandala which is focused on consensus within and without.

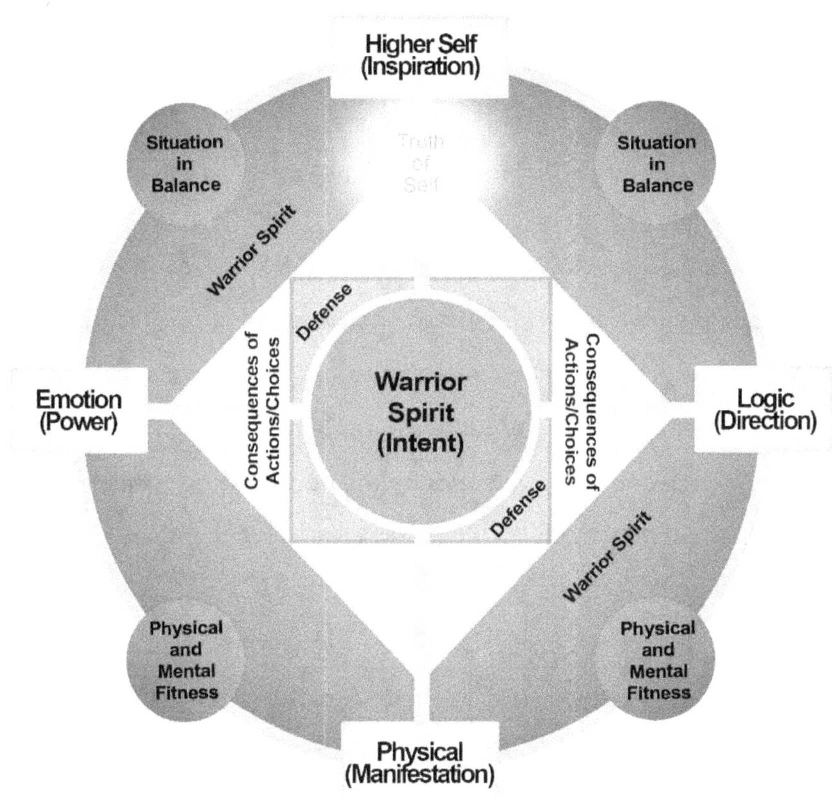

Figure 2

In its most SIMPLE form the two mandalas together would flow like this:

SHADOW	Non-Shadow
Gratification	Emotion
External Validation	Logic

Alphaism   Higher Self

Vanity   Physical/Manifestation

The first pair was Gratification and Emotions. So, let's look from the perspective of the non-shadow Mandala. The Shadow holds Gratification for us as a counterbalance to the emotions.

Now, as we look at the shadow mandala we see some other points that are mirror images of the non-shadow mandala. One of these is the Truth of Self for the light and the Primal core for the shadow. Ok, so, the collective unconsciousness and its shadow and its manifestation is the primal core. Opposite this on the non-shadow mandala is Truth of Self. If you look at the mandala closely you see that there is a light circle of energy above the consequences of actions in the "north" see the quotes before we reach the place of higher self. This is the Truth of self. It is where we have the understanding that is necessary to truly embrace ourselves.

With that as a definition can you see how the primal core is the shadow of it? The primal core is un-manifested will to survive. It is my belief that when we are challenged in the physical world this is where we draw from to act within the flight or fight response. This is the place of that hides our primitive responses.

The truth of self on the other hand is the place where we have integrated and merged and created our own balance to choose a different path.

We said that the Shadow is where we put those things that are not useful to us NOW. And when we need them we can pull them out for usage. We also said that there are times when the shadow takes control if we are not careful and it is this place that is the root of much of the issues with Anger, Bigotry, hatred, within our society. When one feels powerless or out of control and the shadow comes out – this is violence. Fight or we clam up and run away and of course this is flight. Neither of these works well, it is only when we bring the two into balance that we can have reasoned dialog about our differences and mutual respect.

Once we understand this we reach that place of truly being able to manifest ourselves. It is why these two points on the mandalas lead to Higher Self and Alphaism.

These are polar opposite aspects of each of us. The Alphaism is the place where we are selfish, only interested in what we want to accomplish, and don't care how we get there or who we hurt. The higher self on the other hand is only interested in the balance of all. The issue there is that it can manifest sometimes in a way that may be negative to our manifested reality. Ok, so now we put both together and see what happens. The Alpha-ism the selfish, part of ourselves if it is in consensus – remember that – we always come back to consensus – with our higher self then acts in a way that is balanced and harmonious for ourselves.

All of this is a continuum. Do you begin to see how both of these mandalas work together? How they move as both projective and receptive energetically at the same time? How together these are what we call divine.

The next pair is: Manifestation for the non-shadow and Vanity for the shadow. So, Manifestation is what we present for ourselves and others. We manifest our own reality every moment of every day. It is a creative act. SO it is of female energy yet is also male or it is receptive in the creating and projective as we manifest. There are three kinds of vanity:

- Vanity implies the quality of life is important.

- Vanity implies my world is important.

- Vanity implies self-importance.

As we look at how this plays out we see that vanity truly feeds into the Alphaism. It creates an unrealistic expectation that leads inevitably to either self-delusion or a crash. We can see this in our mainstream media too. We hold people up to such a high level that when they fall we turn it into disgust and even hatred. And we are way harder on ourselves than we are on others.

So, Vanity as the opposite of manifestation is an interesting situation. It operates like this:

Manifesting is the manifestation of Divine from within to

without. Vanity is a manifestation of that which is all about me and is a cover up for feelings of inadequacy and low self-esteem.

Interestingly enough Vanity has been spoken of by researchers as the root of much of the issues in our society. It is a shield or cover that hides the truth of self. It is the presentation of a false image hence it is the opposite of manifestation. And who is it that we are actually hiding the truth of self from? Ourselves of course.

People often come to me saying they do not know why they are having such a hard time in life. Often it comes down to what they are manifesting. What they are energetically drawing to themselves. Many times it is Vanity that is causing the issue for them. Remember when we talked about the individuals who are always pointing to their accolades and their "levels" within the craft? These are individuals who have tapped into their own shadow mandala and they get upset when others call them on it because of course, they truly know that they are not what they present.

This issue is one of the reasons back in 2008 we created Three Gates Gathering, (http://threegatesgathering.com) It's mission is to share information on a variety of topics in a non-tradition specific way. It prevents vanity from coming into play. Each year we have 3 topics that are discussed by a specific pair of teachers. Three workshops each one-hour long. Every three years we drop one topic and add another. Here's where the anti-vanity comes in. We choose different teachers from different groups to teach the topics each year. It reminds me of a zen proverb The Empty cup. Do you know the story?

A Zen master was visited by a professor one day who wanted to learn all about Zen. So the Zen master poured him some tea and kept filling the cup. It overflowed and the Zen master kept going. Eventually the professor had enough and asked him to stop because the cup was over full. The Zen master then said – how can you gain new information If your cup is already full. TO learn Zen one must first empty ones cup.

In Western society, we call that being teachable. See how this is a good example? It is our vanity and our me-ism that stops us from learning new things. If we already know everything and are busy proving it to the world then how can we grow?

Three Gates has people come from all over North America. We have traditionalists, eclectics, seekers, and elders from many different groups. In fact in 2017 we had 12 different groups coming all sharing their thirst for knowledge, wisdom and understanding. They tend to come with empty cups to share and learn.

The last aspect is External validation, Most individuals wish at some point to be accepted and have their opinions and deeds recognized. It is a function of how we are members of community, however you define that. It's also where peer pressure comes from, and unfortunately, sometimes overshadows everything else. When external validation is exerting or guiding a person's decisions it can manifest as accepting things that they do not particularly agree. The idea of a mob psychology, or mob behavior can be said to be partially a function of a persons need for external validation. Of course in general this mob psychology has been said to be a function of several social features including deindividualization, a diffusion of responsibility, and anonymity, however within our context I think that an individual is more susceptible to following the crowd, which can lead to mob psychology if they are listening more to their shadow component of External validation.

5 CREATING SHADOW RELATIONSHIPS

A Shadow relationship is defined as one where we project our shadow out to the wider world and choose a person or group of persons that validates one's own shadow. This happens more often than people realize and an awareness of how the shadow contributes to our choices can truly assist in removing many obstacles to good relationships.

Each individual as in last chapter seeks some form of external validation. The saying from Faustus by Mephistopholes – Solamen miseris socios habuisse doloris. (2.1.38-41) "to the unhappy it is a comfort to have had company in misery" or another way - misery loves company is an example of the shadow version of external validation.

This may seem counter-intuitive as are not all people interested in being happy? Well, for the most part, yes. However, if we are wrapped up in our own shadow, then we could think that the way to be happy is to find others who are in their own shadows in the same way. This is what I mean by creating shadow relationships.

Another way people create shadow relationships is by using the toxicity of their relationships to justify their own lack of self-worth. Remember that everything that happens to a person is in that person's control. A person manifests what they desire, even if it comes from the unconscious part of their psyche.

Remembering that humans are social creatures, seeking out like minded individuals is one way that can be indicative of the desire for external validation. John Donne wrote in 1624 in *Devotions upon Emergent Occasions*, meditation 17 part of which goes like this:

'No man is an iland, intire of it selfe; every man is a peece of the Continent, a part of the maine; if a clod bee washed away by the Sea, Europe is the lesse, as well as if a Promontorie were, as well as if a Mannor of thy friends or of thine owne were; any mans death diminishes me, because I am involved in Mankinde; And therefore never send to know for whom the bell tolls; It tolls for thee....

So the key in creating relationships is to first understand within oneself what one is looking for in a relationship. If one is seeking that one's opinions are always validated, then that is what one would find. If what one is looking for is one where one is always challenged, then that is what one would find. If a person is looking for a relationship where they are ALWAYS put first, then that is what they will find.

These three little words, so deceptively simple, yet so life changing. Each of these words is part of the total integration of human experience. Everyone seeks knowledge in some form or another. The development of a child provides an example of how these three aspects interact and integrate.

Children seek knowledge of self, others and the world around them. The infant is only interested in being fed, being dry, and being held. S/He obtains knowledge of self through experimentation and learning to communicate her/his wants and needs. Fairly soon, s/he begins to experience the world of the crib and begins to recognize her/his mother, father and other individuals with whom s/he interact. S/He begins showing emotion in ways other than crying and their elders encourage perceived "good" behaviors. This is an example of KNOWLEDGE being obtained in an infant.

As the child grows, s/he begins to realize when to utilize the skills s/he has learned. Many a mother and father have waited out of sight of a child who will not go to sleep and has learned crying usually results in getting picked up. The new behavior the parents are trying to teach is crying, while appropriate sometimes, is not always the way. The child, on the other hand, begins to see always crying does not get the desired effect and begins experimenting with this new knowledge while learning when to utilize previous knowledge. This is WISDOM.

Finally, as the child enters "school," s/he soon learns not every child has the same level of knowledge or wisdom. Think of the "smart" child who is ostracized by the other children for being different, or liking things most children do not. These children eventually learn to not show certain behaviors and to integrate personal behavior into more "acceptable" ways. This is how s/he utilizes wisdom which makes this UNDERSTANDING.

- Knowledge = What
- Wisdom = When
- Understanding = How

Looking at mythology again we can see in the fourth branch of the Mabinogion there is a really good example of this. In short the part of the story we are interested in is where Gwydion brings Arianrhod the small dark child that is of the result of her crossing over the staff of her brother Math. If you do not know the story, you can look it up in the Mabinogion OR, the fourth branch is prominent in my work <u>Manifesting True Desires: Learning from Arianrhod and the Tree of Life</u> that you can get on alfredwillowhawk.us or on Amazon. In summary, when Gwydyon brings the grown child to Arianrhod, she lays three taboos on the child. Initially it seems terrible she would "punish" a child for the apparent dishonor shown her by Math. After all, what has an innocent child to do with the "embarrassment" of the mother? In modern society, it is inconceivable a child would have anything to do with what the parents have done. However, a closer examination shows, while we do not overtly "punish" children any longer for the "sins" of the parents, they do suffer the consequences of their parent's actions. In discussing the FATE of Gwydyon how do the three taboos serve the purpose of this test?

The three taboos are: 1) No name except what she would give him. 2) No armor unless she give it to him, and 3) no wife of any creature inhabiting the earth.

There is a hint as to the nature of this "small dark child" Gwydyon saves and raises contained in the Bardic tale of Talisen. In Talisen's interactions with the Goddess Ceredwin we find him "ugly". In the writings of the time, a small dark child or an ugly child are not physical descriptors but the karmic attributes of the individuals. As the child Gwydyon raises has no name and is born of the supposed embarrassment of Arianrhod, he stands as the indication of this interaction until the first taboo is lifted. Shakespeare said what is a name? A name is the outward manifestation of the character of the individual. Parents are cautious when naming children, some people are even careful when naming their pets.

If a pet dog is named 'Banshee' and the puppy grows up to be wild, howling all the time and generally destructive, one might wonder at the thoughts of the owner in naming the animal after the banshee. So the unnamed child is "dark" and "small" as it still does not have an indication of the personality he will present.

Some cultures do not name children until their third or fourth birthday as they wait to see what the personality and character of the child is before naming them. In some First Nations cultures, a person is given a name to "hang around the neck" at birth and when the child reaches a particular age to be able to determine her/his own character, as well as demonstrate some of the character either to confirm or choose a new name. So, the "dark" child has no name until such time as his character is demonstrated. Gwydyon had "forced" his own will upon the maiden at Math's feet and hence he decided on his own honor demanded he raise the child on his own. He did not utilize the popular victim mentality and say well she stepped over the staff the child is her responsibility. He raised him as his own then set out to give the child his own life when he went to Arianrhod.

The particular actions utilized are also quite telling. He allowed Arianrhod to watch the child interact on the sidelines when making shoes for her. She noticed he was a sure shot by hitting a wren with his slingshot in the leg. In the myth of the wren, the wren is the king of the birds. She gives him the name Llew, Sure Shot, , is lion which is the "king" of the non-flying animals and recognition of his demonstrated ability. At this point, Arianrhod is also honor bound to accept she had released the taboo by naming the child, again despite the fact she was actually tricked by Gwydyon in the situation. Gwydyon, for his part, never named the child as he honored the terms of the original taboo.

In the society in which they lived, a child became an adult when they received armor and shield. This is the rite of passage to show the child is now responsible for his own actions and no longer under the authority of his parents. In other words, the child is now able to accept the respect of others and of course respect themselves. As Arianrhod gives the boy armor and shield to "defend" the castle from the imagined foes, she is showing she respects the youth and recognizes it is time for him to be an adult. As an adult, all other adults show him respect as he shows it for his family and himself in preparing to defend the castle.

Here are the two characteristics demonstrated in the story thus far – Honor and Respect. Over it all is still a third – Personal Responsibility. Gwydyon accepts the responsibility to raise Llew as part of the root cause of the apparent "dishonor" of his mother Arianrhod.

For our purposes in demonstrating these three taboos as Knowledge, Wisdom, and Understanding, the first taboo – no name except what I give him – knowledge – knowledge of self is in one's name, second taboo – no armor but what I give him – wisdom to know when to "step out" on one's own, and the third taboo – no earthly wife – understanding to pass on the knowledge and wisdom one has obtained.

Honor, respect, and personal responsibility are lessons every individual has learned in their lives. In modern western society, people are constantly told to look outside of themselves for the source of their troubles. It is the economy, Congress, the President, the environment, their parents, anyone but themselves. Advertising companies utilize this socialization to drive consumption to higher and higher levels. If one is only prettier, more handsome, has a better car, the newest cell phone, a bigger house, dress better, anything to promote consumption. Notice all of these things are outward only. An individual can be really well dressed, well-groomed and still be a predator. Many individuals who have long hair, old clothes, and may not have the best personal hygiene will stop to help another human being while the person in the brand new car just drives by, pretending there is no problem. Here is another thing, at least in English. The word is CONSUMPTION – this word means to be consumed or used up. It is also the word used in the past for the disease Tuberculosis where the lungs were consumed by the disease making it impossible for an individual to survive.

The solution is in the word itself, balanced individuals do not seek to consume with no thought to the world around them or even themselves. One really does not need to decimate the planet in the ever increasing desire for more. In fact, as Spiritual Warriors, it behooves us to truly take a stand, and to utilize to the fullest what one has before "buying" new. For me personally, we here at Wite Rayvn are recyclers, and "re-purposers". Even our neighbors know this. In fact a neighbor of ours came over and said that they have a home that needs to come down as it is on a property that was vandalized. We went over this week and began the process. Interestingly enough this is the same neighbor who came over during the Pagan Music Awards and listened to the music after we gave him and his friend a pass for them to listen to that music and the music Friday night at Three Gates Gathering. We did not have an agenda, and we were showing we were part of the community and honored and respected him and accepted him within the confines of what our boundaries were and look where it has gotten us.

This particular property has enough material for us to finish all the projects that are on our list here at the retreat center. Including building a new cabin, creating the storage shed, new porch attached to the totally reconstructed second floor of the barn, the materials are enough for that re-construction as well, as well as some appliances and shoes, clothes, etc that we will share with others.

For our part, we are also helping him by using a cattle gate that was from yet another home that another neighbor asked us to take down for them to help secure the property from vandals.

See, examining these three little words can have a significant impact in all behavior in the context of one's individual life, family, and community. Earlier it was stated Understanding was the how. Honor, respect and personal responsibility are the working out of the How.

If every action is predicated by the examination of these three powerful words, our lives will be much more in balance with the universe around us.

Honor – ourselves and others

Respect – ourselves and others

Personal Responsibility – WE are the cause of our OWN actions.

. Earlier it was stated Understanding was the how. Honor, respect and personal responsibility are the working out of the How.

If every action is predicated by the examination of these three powerful words, our lives will be much more in balance with the universe around us.

Honor – ourselves and others

Respect – ourselves and others

Personal Responsibility – WE are the cause of our OWN actions.

Most children are taught to "own up" to personal mistakes and accept the consequences of those actions. How is it, as adults we push this teaching away and blame everyone else for problems? A balanced individual always takes responsibility for personal actions.

As we take responsibility for our actions, it is important to not fall into the trap of JUDGEMENT. No human being has all the information necessary to judge another.

How many times do individuals tell us we are WRONG or attribute motives to our actions we ourselves would never have thought of? Here is an imaginary conversation between two domestic partners which is reflective of many of the interactions of daily life.

(Scene) Partner 1 is doing dishes in the kitchen while Partner 2 is sitting in the living room, out of sight, playing a video game)

Partner 1: Honey, could you please take out the garbage it is full and In my way.

Partner 2: WHAT? DO YOU THINK I DON'T DO ANYTHING AROUND HERE? I WORK ALL DAY JUST LIKE YOU, I MADE THE BED THIS MORNING; I SET THE TABLE NOW I SIT DOWN TO RELAX AND IT'S A PROBLEM FOR YOU???

If Partner 1 responds to the comment by Partner 2, a fight begins. This is an example of self-judgment and projection. Partner 2 has some doubts about her/his own actions while Partner 1 is still working on domestic tasks and lashes out at Partner 1, attributing this self-judgment to the partner.

Examining the actions of Partner 2 and holding them up to Honor, Respect, and personal responsibility we can see there could be a possible disconnect. No one can determine whether actions are honorable, or respectful because anything we as individuals OUTSIDE of PARTNER 2 determine, is JUDGEMENT.

If we establish we as individuals only act on our own honor codes and allow others to determine their own honor codes, we might see a better more balanced peaceful world.

In the first chapter I spoke of an old bumper sticker from the 70's which reads, "Guns don't kill people. People kill people." This is true. The weapon does not have a mind of its own, determined to leap into the first available and shoot itself. It takes an individual to determine s/he will shoot the weapon. Many of society's laws are based on the judgment of a few, determining what is best for all. This is directly opposed to the concepts discussed here.

In order to work at being non-judgmental, I utilize another saying – It's Not My Problem. Anything I can not directly control is NOT MY PROBLEM. It makes for a more balanced life.

Think about it, if I am driving down the road and there is someone driving very fast behind me, I pull over and let them pass. I do not slow down to control the behavior. Maybe they are rushing to the hospital or home because a child is sick. I have no idea what is going on – and it is not my problem. I can choose to make it more difficult or easier on myself – so I pull over and let them pass.

Some might say this is cruel. No, it is being true to my own honor code and showing respect for choices of another. It does not mean I would stand by and let someone get beaten up, raped or subjected to violence   when this is clearly interfering with the free will of another individual; it just means I do not JUDGE the actions of another which are not directly seeking to control me – besides – ITS NOT MY PROBLEM.

As I said earlier in the Mabinogion, Llew and Gwydyon do not spend hours seeking to blame Arianrhod for their "problems." They simply work it out for themselves and move forward. This is the key for us as we look at our relationships. SO, Shadow Relationships you can see where we have been going I am sure. When one "feels something" for a new person, that indescribable excitement, racing of the heart, dilation of the pupils, besides the physiological connection between chemo-receptors and pheromones, there is the vibration from each person – that seems to mingle and become one. It validates something that one feels is missing within themselves as we are looking for completeness. Of course, this may seem good. The issue is when what we are seeking is coming from a place of shadow enhancement.

Shadow enhancement is that which emanates from one of a person's shadow elements at least and at most from one's desire to strengthen one's own ego. This is neither white nor black – it is grey.

The next thing to remember is that there is no judgment of self when this happens. Sometimes it is important to have a shadow enhancement, especially when what is magnified in the relationship is something that has been placed in the shadow temporarily. For example, one individual places their ability to speak their opinion in their shadow due to a plethora of experiences in their lives. They find a person who encourages them to speak their mind and accepts their opinion so the individual who has placed this behavior in their shadow now feels comfortable speaking their opinion. I have seen this situation many times in my time as a spiritual coach.

On the other hand, if that same person who has placed their ability to speak their opinion in their shadow gravitates toward a person who is "always right" in their own mind, and makes sure that everyone knows it, then it is validating the shadow aspect in the first person.

In the above scenario what happens when the first person begins to work on themselves and begins to integrate, and strengthen the very aspect that drew them towards their partner? Right, as they begin to share their opinion and disagreement ensues, they become uncomfortable in the relationship. In the worst-case scenario, eventually as they develop their ability to speak, and modify their boundaries then the relationship begins to fall apart. This is one of the reasons that I do not truly believe in the concept of a soul mate. Well I believe that the vibrational patterns of individuals that gravitate toward each other is some sort of soul mate, however, as one's vibrational pattern changes, then the synchronicity of the vibrational patterns may become dis-harmony, and hence the relationship becomes troubled.

When couples have open communication in a real way, with mutual honor, respect, and personal responsibility then they can work through those differences as they grow together. If one partner is growing and changing and the other is not then ultimately there is a disconnect in the relationship that can lead to dissolution at least, and violence at worst.

This is what we mean by Shadow Relationships. Many people have had shadow relationships in their lives. I think that some of the divorces that have occurred in marriages are due to this. It is a mistaken understanding of the feelings and vibrational simpatico between individuals that cause individuals to create situations for themselves and to ultimately create shadow relationships that are not in their best interests. These shadow relationships serve as a reminder of everything that a person is struggling with within themselves, and reinforces the very things that they are working through in a physical manifested way.

There is a saying – Son's marry their mothers, and daughters marry their fathers. While I do not agree particularly with this statement it does serve as a reminder that those things that are part of our choices, defenses, and desires come out as part of how we were raised and what our experiences have been in our lives.

6 ACCEPTING CONSEQUENCES

Now that there is a framework for how shadow relationships form it is important for each individual to practice acceptance of the consequences of our own actions. Yes, remember each individual is in control of their choices and takes responsibility for their own actions. Once one takes responsibility for their own actions it is the consequences of those actions that need acceptance as well. Remember there are no victims only those who refuse to accept the consequences of their own actions.

Actions means every choice we make, every change we facilitate, every word that we speak. The consequences of those actions are the same. The spiritual warrior is in total control of their actions and the consequences of those actions.

At this level of understanding one has absolute control instantly over their universe. It's a great place to be. I mean it's an intriguing place to be, I mean it's an interesting place to be, I mean… Oh you can decide for yourself what kind of place this is. The important thing to remember is that this is the place where all things are possible and all things happen. Period.

I was having a conversation with an associate of mine after we worked together on a particularly difficult situation – the details of which are unimportant- and some of the people were surprised by the outcome of the situation and we were saddened that those individuals do not understand the consequences of their own actions. It is also true that the universe will not accept a void, there is always an action and a consequence to that action. While the situation was going on facts were illuminated, objectively, the party that was being acted against did not RE-act to the situation only continued their actions and ultimately there was the push back and those who sought negative against another instead received negative themselves.

Think about it. What goes out comes back. If you project negativity then negativity is what is attracted to you. Let's look within our current context at this.

So it works both ways here. In this case one projects energy out to the universe, these projections once away are attracted to that which is receptive to that energy. Over time the projection is received by more and more "entities" and builds up until it is projected out to the next receiver. In fact it goes out and in and encompasses way more than what or whom it was intended too.

This is one of the reasons that for myself I am very careful what I project to others. A true balanced individual will analyze the information that comes to them, and reach that wonderful consensus within and then take action accordingly. For myself I choose to not take direct negative action on another, I do protect myself, but I am way too strong within myself to be controlled by another.

Yes, you heard me. Controlled by another. I hear the questions on the ether. How is doing active work against one who comes against me giving up control. It is my experience that most people want to be in harmony and balance within themselves. The key here is that one who is working on balancing the shadow and non-shadow aspects of themselves and making informed choices for actions.

The fully aware individual is cognizant and operates here. The primary drive is no longer themselves it encompasses all that is around them. You can see it in their daily lives. In the choices they make, and how they move through their days.

I want to introduce a new concept - the Spiritual Warrior. All of the work that we have been doing within ourselves in this book can be said to be the work of the Spiritual Warrior as a kind of self-healing. One of the major aspects of the Spiritual Warrior and their work on themselves was removing the sources of dis-ease. So, a Spiritual Warrior is also a healer.

I don't mean a doctor or even that this is their focus yet, just like every warrior on the battle field has some knowledge of First Aid every spiritual warrior has the tools to Heal themselves and if they choose by their direct choices to help others to heal themselves.

This is the key here. They are facilitators of their own and others healing. Every day the Spiritual Warrior has the opportunity to help others to recognize the very lessons that they have learned. This is another way that one can project energy that one has received. In some disciplines this is called gratitude.

When I started my studies in Metaphysics I was taught to say And So It Is when I finished a meditation or a working. This statement has two sides to it.

Then first is acknowledging that the situation has already been completed. In Orthodox Judaism at the very beginning of the Yom Kipper service, one of the high holy days of the Jewish faith, the Rabbi or leader of the prayers starts off with a blessing that when translated says: Thank you Creator for manifesting our desired ends for this day.

The second side of the statement is recognition and blessing for the universe's contribution to what we desire. See, we are all part of the totality of the Universe. We are not alone. There is no loneliness, only choice. Reach out into the collective consciousness of the universe and accept that which it has to offer. You are in control there is no reason for unhappiness, they are something that we create, we manifest and we can stop. This is how we can first manifest as a healer a self-healer.

I was talking with someone whom I had just met who said I had really calm and positive energy. I thanked them and then they asked an interesting question. They said they did not understand how I could have a radio show called The Warrior Within when my energy was so peaceful and calm. I thought about it for a while and realized that many people see Warrior as opposite peace. It reminds me of many a conversation I have had with Veterans and Warriors of Indigenous peoples. Each veteran and each warrior or brave if you will knows that calmness is better than manifested anger, and balance is one of the keys to survival on the battle field.

Our lives can be considered a battlefield. All the in this book and others that you use in our lives are how we can be at peace within ourselves.

Do we succeed all the time, maybe yes and maybe no. What's the difference, none. Each person walks their own path. Each person makes their own choices. Each person accepts their own consequences for their own actions.

Heal yourself, walk quietly, not boastfully, this is where we stand as balanced individuals who make good choices for ourselves.

In the Warrior Within Release program I have created with the help of others two mandalas to help focus on the aspects of ourselves to create balance. These two mandalas called the shadow mandala and the non-shadow mandala are introduced later in this book. The two mandalas can be used as the tool of opening up to a new understanding of our personal temples. Here is something that was written by someone who is working through the Warrior Within Release program that has bearing on this chapter.

The mandala has become a scale model of that temple, where I can gather all of my emotional faces to one point, muster all of my intellectual ones at another. I see my physical faces, my senses, my filters, and all of my meditations associated with physical stimuli orient in one large area. I see myself at the center. Bast is always at the temple in my meditations and seems to know what to do when I am at a loss. Given her knowledge, I would say that she acts as the set of rods that runs through all things, the "higher self." I've never seen the Temple so organized before. I now have a tool for understanding what I'm seeing and doing, in a sense. And I can interact with it or at least, take a closer look at what is really happening when something seems amiss. ..this leads to all kinds of questions to meditate on...

I see the Warrior Within program as a common-language, common sense, all access approach for climbing out of "hell" and getting on the path to "heaven" with our understanding of those terms being defined as above. I don't believe there is any one way on the Path. But it does seem as if you've been able to help remove a few of the extra faces, find some short cuts, and make it less scary. The radio show is good at finding a common language. It really draws upon a lot of different schools, and I enjoy that.

I am humbled by this individuals take on the mandala and I share it here as an encouragement for each and every reader to utilize the Mandala in their own work, in their own way.

If we look at the Mandala as the realization of the connection between the outside (chaos) and inside (order) the pathways are a way to make sense of all the myriad of emotions and words that come at us every second of every day.

Taking the next step in this, we see the projective and receptive energy as two poles of our existence.

Just as a convenience let us say that female = receptive and male = projective and these two aspects of energy work together in many aspects of our lives. Ok, so first news flash. We each have within us BOTH projective and receptive energy. Yea, surprise, surprise. When we are in our mother's womb at first we have the potential to be physically male or female. It is at about 18 weeks that the gender of the fetus is first recognizable. What has been going on earlier than this? Is the fetus then androgynous? Maybe, at least energetically it is, in my opinion. I also do not think that even after gender differentiation that we lose that ability to connect with both receptive and projective energy.

Do we not receive energy from the world around us? As spiritual beings, this is even more evident. In the meditation connect with the Universal Consciousness on my CD *Meditations for Life* we step into the place of recognition of ourselves as cosmic beings. Even Western Faiths admit that God or the Divine is both male and female – projective and receptive.

Many individuals get caught up in the gender specification of our physical bodies and forget that to receive or project is what is going on in our lives every day! Imagine for a minute if an individual only received. What would happen? They would take in energy and take in energy and take in energy, I suppose eventually they would explode or begin to dis-assemble from all the intake. It would be similar to a bottle of water being heated up on the stove without any release valve. Boy, would that be a mess during canning!

What about the other way? If an individual never received but was always projecting energy, what would happen when all their energy was gone? Would they shrivel up and disappear?

Yea, it's always the Middle Way, we project and receive constantly. So, if we are in the middle way, and in control of our own actions, then to use a phrase that some of my students use – It's time for a little "adult-ing"; meaning that acceptance of the consequences of our actions and moving forward with them is how we grow as spiritual warriors and balanced individuals who make good choices in their relationships.

No one is responsible for any other individual except themselves. However, I choose to be part of the balance and harmony of others, my community, and the global society. – That is the point. I choose to be part of it and I respect and honor it enough to allow others to have the same control of themselves as I have of myself. I look at others the way I want to be looked at. Furthermore, it does not matter what others think or do, as long as it does not impact my balance and harmony. If it does then- the tools of the Spiritual Warrior are utilized to "end" the battle.

The key is that the battle also is the war. So, as a Spiritual Warriors and balanced individuals the way to win the war is to end the battle always with the actions one chooses.

As we build relationships that are either shadow or non-shadow we are actually choosing to either evolve or de-evolve. Even though each individual exists separately within their own creation, there is still the interactions and the influence of all the other creations that are the separate realities of each person.

Let's think about what Evolution actually means. I do not mean in the Darwinian sense. Here is a beginning point.

According to the Oxford Dictionary Evolution is *the gradual development of something and devolution is the act of giving power from a central authority or government to an authority or a government in a local region.*

Bet you did not know that. The important thing in this definition for us is "the act of giving power to something else". We might even make up our own word **de-evolution** to keep a clear picture of what imagery we are creating for the framework of our discussion. OK, so the essence here is that when we evolve we move to a "new level". And when we de-evolve we move to a "new level". Wait, isn't that the same?

Yes it is. It's a matter of the direction we are moving in and from where within we are operating. We have the aspect of non-shadow and we have the aspect of Shadow or our Id which for us is the more primal ego driven self.

Now, remember also, no judgment here, when one is operating from the aware and balanced perspective and not the Shadow perspective then I propose that we are evolving.

Those times that we operate from the perspective of the Shadow then we are de-evolving. See, still a balance. Yes., there is a balance between the shadow and non-shadow. This balance must be maintained or there can be no movement.

This is a continuing process there is no stagnation. Think about a pendulum in a vacuum. Once set in motion if there are no other outside influences the pendulum will swing from one end of its arc to another for as long as no other influence is placed upon it.

This is the existence that we live in. We are like that pendulum swinging between Shadow and non-shadow and it is the arc that movement prescribes that is our total internal balance. It is the way that we hear and can process information within the chaos we call the universe.

This puts a different spin on manifestation. There is a school of thought that says we manifest our own reality. However, what are we allowing to influence us as we manifest that reality. Remember that the key is that the battle also is the war. So, as a balanced individual the way to win the war is to end the battle always with the actions that they are based on the one's own choices.

As we begin to explore the concept of SELF EVOLUTION vs SELF DEVOLUTION we can see how once again it is our actions that set our own course. We are the navigator of our own existence as balanced individuals and when we choose to allow others to influence us when we choose to allow our own Shadow to influence us – we devolve.

In many circles, there is talk about changing and increasing our vibrational pattern in order to become closer to that which we call divine. Let us look at what choices we can make as balanced individuals to increase that vibrational pattern toward the divine within and without. Another way of looking at "changing the vibrational pattern" is Coming closer to God or God Consciousness.

In, Carl Jung's "Answer to Job," Psychology and Religion, CW 11, par. 658.

The continuing, direct operation of the Holy Ghost on those who are called to be God's children implies, in fact, a broadening process of incarnation. Christ, the son begotten by God, is the first-born who is succeeded by an ever-increasing number of younger brothers and sisters.

These are, however, neither begotten by the Holy Ghost nor born of a virgin. . .. Their lowly origin (possibly from the mammals) does not prevent them from entering into a close kinship with God as their father and Christ as their brother.

Later he says in "Letter to Pèe Lachat," The Symbolic Life, CW 18, par. 1551. *[There is a] . . . continued and progressive divine incarnation. Thus man is received and integrated into the divine drama. He seems destined to play a decisive part in it; that is why he must receive the Holy Spirit.*

I look upon the receiving of the Holy Spirit as a highly revolutionary fact which cannot take place until the ambivalent nature of the Father is recognized. If God is the summum bonum, the incarnation makes no sense, for a good god could never produce such hate and anger that his only son had to be sacrificed to appease it.

A Midrash says that the Shofar is still sounded on the Day of Atonement to remind YHWH of his act of injustice towards Abraham (by compelling him to slay Isaac) and to prevent him from repeating it.

A conscientious clarification of the idea of God would have consequences as upsetting as they are necessary. They would be indispensable for an interior development of the trinitarian drama and of the role of the Holy Spirit.

The Spirit is destined to be incarnate in man or to choose him as a transitory dwelling-place. "Non habet nomen proprium," says St. Thomas; because he will receive the name of man.

That is why he must not be identified with Christ. We cannot receive the Holy Spirit unless we have accepted our own individual life as Christ accepted his.

Thus we become the "sons of god" fated to experience the conflict of the divine opposites, represented by the crucifixion.

OK, so to move this out of the realm of the Abrahamic faiths – what Jung is saying here is that the Divine, however we define it for ourselves, as we strive to vibrate faster or stronger or dare I say higher as in frequency then we enter into kinship or become more like that which we perceive as Divine.

Also that the balance of shadow and non-shadow is the proof of our higher frequency or as he says the "sons of god" fated to experience the conflict of the divine opposites.

This also answers a question that comes up many times in a person's life. Why do bad things keep happening to me? I work on my intents, I work on my development but I keep getting tripped up!

Well, maybe these are not "trip ups" at all! Maybe it is just resetting the balance within or it is part of the evolutionary process of the balanced individual. In an article called *Tension of the Opposites* by Paul Levy he states as follows and its really eloquent.

Jung makes the point that we are only able to creatively hold the tension of the opposites if we realize that the opposites themselves are manifestations of the Self and are not of the ego. Recognizing this will allow us to not identify with either of the opposites as well as to disidentify with the conflict itself, and by doing this we will be clearing the space for the solution to come. This is the birth of the Self, which is none other than the incarnation of God in and through us. By consciously going through this real life passion play, or in Jung's words, a "divine drama," we become a conduit for the incarnating Godhead itself, which Jung realized was the greatest service that we could do for the divine. This is what Jung meant when he talked about "a broadening process of incarnation," "the continuing incarnation of God," and "the Christification of the many." This is why he defined individuation, the process of becoming whole, as incarnation, for to the extent that we claim our wholeness we allow God to incarnate in this world.

SO, The balanced individual is the Self which is the Divine within. We know that the Divine in all its manifestation is both within and without. We as a collective or universal consciousness have manifested the energy we call divine. So, as balanced individuals we connect with that part of ourselves which is divine.

This then is the SELF-Awareness. Jens B. Asendorpf Veronique Warkentin and Pierre-Marie Baudonniere in their work *Self-Awareness and Other-Awareness II: Mirror Self-Recognition, Social Contingency Awareness, and Synchronic Imitation* used the work of Lewis and Brooks-Gun (1979) where they applied a red dot to an infant's nose and then held the child up to a mirror. Children who recognized themselves in the mirror would reach for their own noses rather than the reflection in the mirror, indicating that they had at least some self-awareness. In their hypothesis from a brain chemistry perspective the researchers believe that an area of the brain known as the anterior cingulate, in the frontal lobe region, plays an important role in developing self-awareness. The Lewis and Brooks-Gun experiment suggests that self-awareness begins to emerge in children around the age of 18 months, an age that coincides with the rapid growth of spindle cells in the anterior cingulate. Researchers have also used brain imaging to show that this region becomes activated in adults who are self-aware.

I contend that self is something that grows and matures as the child matures and as balanced individuals when we combine the concept that the divine is within and without and the collective recognition of that divine of humanity as a whole leads us to the conclusion that the balanced individual and the Self and the Divine are if not a trinity they are at least a three strand cord to our own spiritual development.

OK, so we have spoken a lot about the evolution of balanced individual. There is as we said earlier the concept of de-evolution or devolution even though the term devolution is not typically used in this fashion. This is when we do not build effective consensus within ourselves and the shadow takes primacy. This still creates a balance, but it is a balance that is also lowering of the vibration pattern or a lowering of the frequency. When this happens of course other lower vibrational entities begin to gravitate toward us just like when it is a higher vibrational pattern that higher frequency entities gravitate toward us.

The de-evolution is not a done deal. Remember the pendulum? There is a definite swing or arc between the lowest and highest point. Since no one exists in a vacuum like a pendulum in the physical world we have actions and pressures that operate on us. It is important for balanced harmonious individuals to make sure that as we swing between the poles of our existence – Evolution or De-Evolution that we utilize our consensus building skills to raise our own vibrational frequency so that even when the external and internal interference happens to lower that frequency that we have the proverbial tuning forks to raise our frequency again. Imagine it as a spiral moving ever upward toward the unification with the divine and all other aspects of divine.

As one seeks to create relationships with others, remembering that you are a divine image at least, if not truly divine within yourself, then you are seeking not something to balance your shadow, but something to enhance your non-shadow.

7 CHAOS AND COSMOS

Relationships are messy. In fact we could almost say that they are chaotic. This is interesting because as we have seen in previous chapters humans as social creatures look to form relationships.

According to the Cambridge English Dictionary Chaos is defined as: *a state of disorder and confusion.* This is an ok place to begin. However, I want to add another word to Chaos and that is Chaos theory, and a qualifier, to that – in psychology. So, let's look at Chaos theory in psychology. Ok so first we can say that Chaos Theory is a branch of mathematics that reflects an interdisciplinary theory stating that within the apparent randomness of chaotic complex systems, there are underlying patterns, constant feedback loops, repetition, self-similarity, fractals, self-organization, and reliance on programming at the initial point known as sensitive dependence on initial conditions.

Psychologically we can say that chaos theory is a way to understand the apparent randomness and the underlying pattern we as individuals or societies seek to create, support, and maintain.

There is another aspect of chaos; it is that which is absorbed by the individual. Think about how a balanced individual acknowledges each aspect of themselves, and integrates them to manifest something I call the true spiritual warrior. According to the article The Psychological Significance of Chaos and Disorder by Jonathan Marshall in the *Canberra Jung Society Newsletter Autumn 2011* the author states that:

the 'butterfly effect' has relevance. This asserts not just that we cannot predict the results of things with accuracy, because of lack of knowledge, but that different degrees of accuracy in our measurements of the same events, may give completely different results. We might normally expect that as we get more accurate data, we would converge towards a particular result, however in a sufficiently complex interactive system, increasing accuracy of measurements may result in entirely different results. As a consequence, some things are inherently unpredictable and thus chaotic; they escape predictable order. I would say that it is obvious that human beings and human systems are complex and interactive in this sense, and thus tend to subvert our predictions, and thankfully so. There is always potential for surprise in life – good or bad – and life always escapes our exact plans. Indeed, the more exact those plans are the more our life will tend to escape them.

If we think about how the flowers and plants that were planted at the Wite Rayvn Retreat Center© from all over North America and how they have grown and not grown, as well as the indigenous plants and herbs that are on the property, looking at how they seem to grow together, and have a mind of their own shows this as well. In fact, there are times that plants "mysteriously" show up in the center of gardens, and other times, plants that might not seem to be able to grow together according to the traditional wisdom do just fine some years and other years not so fine.

Dr. Marshall continues saying:

Chaos in human psychology can be looked at simplistically as: ego equals order, and unconscious equals disorder. The order of the ego is both the order we impose or discover in ourselves and the order we impose upon, or discover, in the world. The unconscious is everything else: That which escapes our order, that which is created by our ordering and subverts that order, That which our ordering leads us to ignore, and That which is completely beyond our conception but which still affects us. The unconscious resists our ordering. Many processes are unconscious – not only psychological, physical or biological processes, but social and ecological ones. Jung would later call this wider system which seeks balance 'the Self'. But here, the important point is that the unconscious is collective and plural. There is nothing singular about these processes, and there is no need to assume they are always in harmony, or can be reconciled – hence they can appear, feel, or be, chaotic and disordering.

Individuals while always **in control of self, are also apparently out of control**. This brings us to our purpose within ourselves and our relationships. It seems sometimes that our relationships are out of our control. Like the weather. Each relationship when looked at through the lens of what we think it should and should not be, should and should not do is uncontrollable and hence chaotic. However, if we look at it from the place of Chaos itself, the receptive, all embracing, disorder of the world, from our perspective, we see that it is that which allows us to grow, change, and accept ourselves and others. Relationships are not controllable, after all we are not automatons that follow a program. Each program if you will within us is different, ever hear the saying – everyone marches to a different drummer? Yea, that's it. So, if within we march to a different drummer – and by that, I mean that each aspect of ourselves has a different opinion on what is the perfect solution to any issue, think about all the individuals and all their aspects it's a wonder that any agreement occurs!

Cosmos as a theory is known as cosmology. So, looking at science and physics we have several modern and postmodern definitions for Cosmos or cosmology. The citation for this is: http://www.physicsoftheuniverse.com/cosmological.html. There is one definition of Cosmos that fits nicely with our discussion in this chapter.

Multiverse –

The Russian-American physicist Andrei Linde developed the inflationary universe idea further in 1983 with his chaotic inflation theory (or eternal inflation), which sees our universe as just one of many "bubbles" that grew as part of a multiverse owing to a vacuum that had not decayed to its ground state.

If we look at each individual as one of the bubbles of the multiverse then looking at the big picture all the bubbles they seem to be in chaos, yet internally each bubble is a cosmos. The cosmos projects itself or makes itself known to other cosmos' and the interactions of each cosmos creates an order that is different from each of the individual cosmos'.

This is what we are as individuals and individuals within these relationships. Acceptance of our partners despite the differences that are apparent or real, allows for interaction at a peaceful and harmonious manner. This is the key to living and thriving in relationships and how to avoid shadow relationships.

After all each individual in the relationship chose to be in that relationship. Of course, as we said earlier as the controller of your own cosmos, you also have the ability to change and grow as a couple. There are some relationships that start off well even if they are based on a shadow vibration. If both parties are willing to communicate effectively then they can both grow and the relationship grows stronger.

However, if only one party is changing, then a different solution eventually becomes apparent.

There is another more serious kind of shadow relationship and that is the toxic relationship. This is a relationship that reinforces the shadow of both parties. It is akin to what we called the mob psychology in a previous chapter. The constant reinforcement of the shadow aspects of each partner lead to a downward spiral toward oblivion.

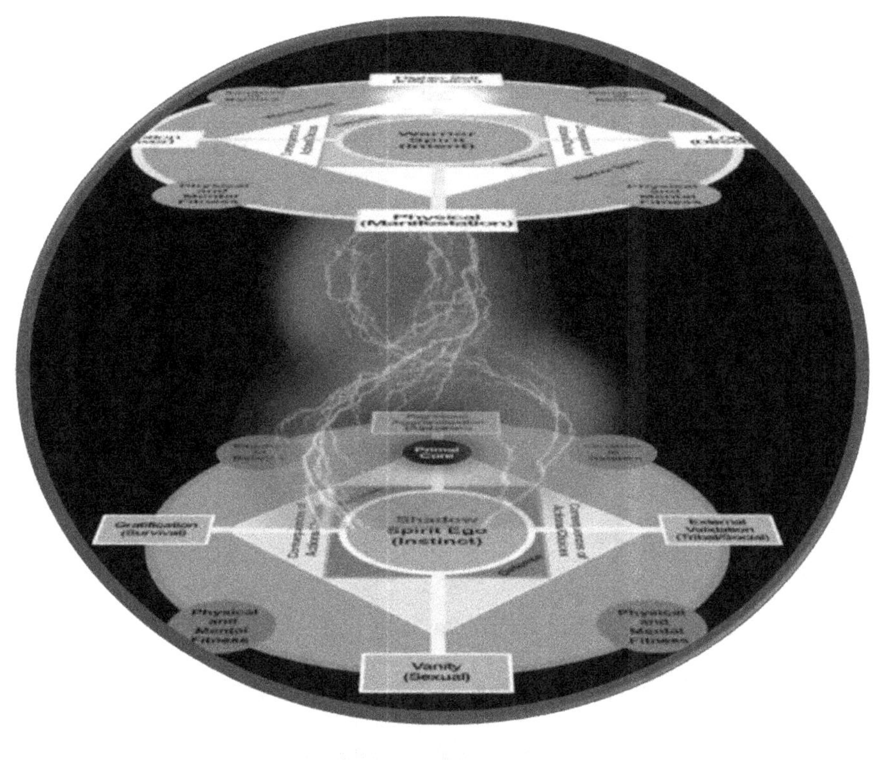

8 TOXIC OR NOT TOXIC

One of the issues with Shadow relationships is that they often result in toxic relationships. A toxic relationship as we said at the end of the last chapter is one where the reinforcement of shadow is so complete that it begins a cycle of enhancement of those shadow characteristics for each individual. This reinforcement becomes so complete that it totally overshadows any positive that the relationship has accomplished.

Individuals act according to the information that they receive from both internal and external stimuli. Each individual has a logical component of their being. Let's take a look at what happens when a stimuli or information is received from outside ourselves.

OK, so first, remember that we receive information from outside of ourselves through the five senses. Each of these stimuli are then received, interpreted or disregarded in our cognitive or logical "brain" then we act upon that stimuli.

Second, if we utilize our mandalas the non-shadow we have logical, physical, emotional and higher self which feed or maintain the balanced individual. In the Shadow mandala we have the Tribal/Social or external Validation., Vanity or sexual drive, Gratification/Survival, and Alphaism that feed or maintain the Instinct or Shadow Spirit/Ego.

Third, neither of these entities, our shadow and non-shadow or exist by themselves. They are interconnected and fuel each other in a feedback loop that is our total existence. This is how we interpret our internal and external world in order to make the decisions that result in our own behaviors.

The logical aspect or component of ourselves interprets the external stimuli. As there is always some form of consensus or communication between the two mandalas this is also received by the external validation part of the shadow mandala. Now, once that information is received it is then interpreted by the External Validation part of the Shadow mandala and then the decision or interpretation of External Validation acts as the fuel for the action that is taken.

Now, this is an oversimplification because all the aspects of each of the mandala's play their part, however, this is an example of how the process works within ourselves.

We also know that within the universe energy is either projective or receptive. Imagine conduits or pathways between the shadow and non-shadow mandala or aspects of ourselves. These conduits can be considered communication points that move in both directions. When the energy is going into the shadow it is a non-shadow conduit and when the information is coming from the shadow it is a shadow conduit. This is important and seems counter intuitive. However, as it is one conduit that is bi-directional it depends on which aspect of ourselves is projecting and which aspect of ourselves is receiving that determines the "ownership" of the conduit. This ownership is important as it is part of how we interpret the information that we are receiving and how we decide to act or how we control ourselves. In this scenario, the conduit for the logical brain is a shadow conduit, which is projective and pushing the information onto the non-shadow and the outer world.

OK, so to finish out this particular oversimplified example. The information is projected from the logical mind to the shadow aspect of External Validation, there it is processed feeds our Shadow .

Instinct and then sends or projects back to the non-shadow mandala that people will not like me – and if the shadow is in control – the action we choose to take is shadow controlled.

OK, so it's a little more complicated than this. Picture this if you will.

The Shadow and the Non-Shadow are in communication. Picture the two mandala's as representations of Shadow and Non- Shadow. Now, visualize the Shadow Mandala underneath the non-shadow Mandala..

Now, picture conduits like electrical conduits between the Center of the Non-Shadow Mandala – the balanced individual or spiritual warrior and the Shadow Mandala – Our Ego/Instinct/ID.

This conduit is created by the consensus of each of the aspects of each of the aspects. So, it is not smooth, it is a interwoven structure that has the individual feeds from each aspect of ourselves.

So on the non-shadow within each individual which is the combination of the Physical, Emotional, Logical and Higher aspects of ourselves.

On the Shadow within each individual which is the combination of the Vanity/Sexual, Survival, Alphaism, and Tribal/Social aspects. See Figure 3 on the next page. (Note: <u>IF you purchased this book legally you also have the electronic color plates of figure 1, 2, and 3 that I personally send each person after purchase</u>.)

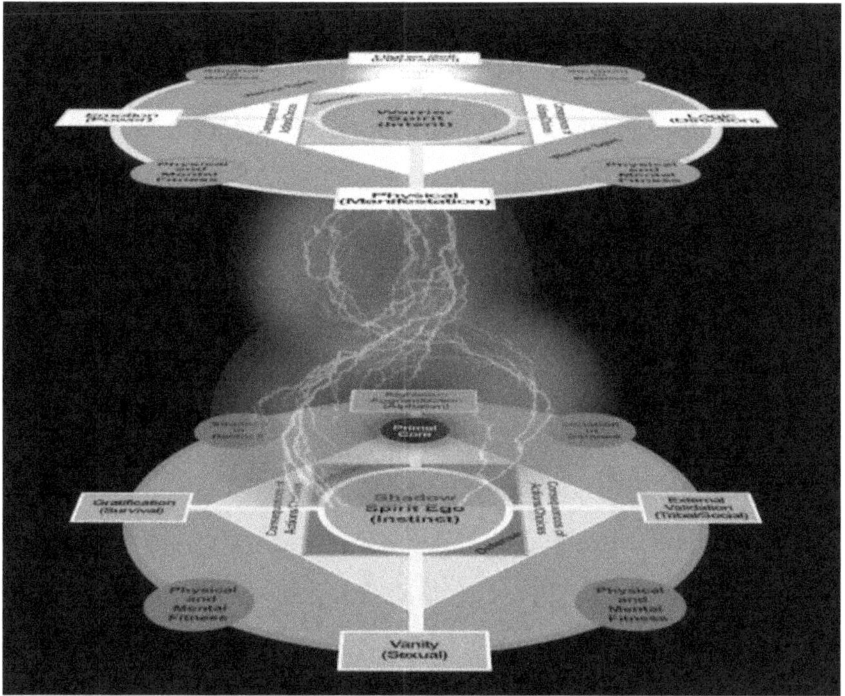

Figure 3

OK, so for all the visual type people here is a way to look at each of these strands that make up the conduit. We can assign colors to each of the strands. Coming out of the non-shadow Mandala Physical – green, Emotional – blue, Logical - red, Higher -white or purple.

Coming out of the Shadow Mandala sexual/vanity – Red, Survival- Green, Alphaism – Black, External Validation – Blue.

I have particular reasons for choosing these colors as these colors vibrate at particular wavelengths that are similar to the energy of each of these aspects of ourselves.

If we assign these colors to these particular strands then when the "primary controller" of a particular decision making process is not from the consensus then these colors on the conduit are brighter. See, a mnemonic device to help us see what aspect of ourselves we are listening to better.

Now, all of this is for us to understand how we act and interact with others. If an individual finds themselves reacting then **the act** of **reacting** projects to the non-shadow mandala, and makes the determination of the action. Notice what words I emphasized here. Even when one re-acts or allows outside influence to "make the decision for us" it is **still an action and a choice**! However, in this case the shadow is dominant.

The mechanism for this in this scenario is that if one is reacting **the external validation cord of the shadow mandala is feeding into the emotional branch (I want to feel good) of the non-shadow Mandala and then that feedback loop overpowers the balanced action!**

This is where the issues with toxic relationships. What happens next is that one partner gets upset – see another emotional response – with themselves and pulls away from the individual with whom they have allowed to control them.

Have you had incidences in your own lives where a person who has been working with you, or associating with you decides that you are not a good fit for them anymore? Even though you have not altered what or how you have interacted with them? If you are fortunate the person at least gives you some reason why they are separating from you. Now, here comes the hard part. Even when that person says they want nothing to do with you – there are still interactions that come up. Unless you or they move to another planet. This is how toxic relationships end.

All individuals on this little ball vibrate and rotate and revolve around each other to some extent at some time, and those times happen more often than you expect. Have you seen that in your own lives? Many times in my life I thought that a person was "out of my life" only to have them swing back around and be within my awareness once again. Now, not burning those bridges, not speaking gossip, but recognizing your own part in the dissolution of that particular relationship allows for the ability to be "civil" with that person at least.

In order to change a toxic relationship into a non-toxic relationship there are several things that an individual can do. I hear the question = What if a person is actually out to discredit, or make issues for you?

My answer – so what

There we have it. This is the key. Now, how others perceive that behavior is of course not my problem! If people are tapping into their own shadows and their own fears, then that is their choice. There are times when people who seem to be "with you" are really not with you. They are seeking the external validation of your agreement with their interpretation of the events or situation. It is very important as spiritual warriors that we understand and utilize all our tools.

It's true that many people fall subject to this. Their own need for external validation drives them to seem to change their opinion and to disregard their own experiences with individuals and accept somebody else's experience as the true experience. I for one, trust me more than I trust other. Even when I first meet someone, I begin by expecting that they are as they present themselves and operate within that, not what any other person says. Once I have a relationship with a person, if someone else is trying to change my opinion or relationship with someone I first examine and gather the necessary facts to see all the sides of their relationship with the person they are speaking about. See, boundaries and limits.

OK, so the next step is to realize that my boundaries and my limits are just that. mine. I do not need to announce to the world what those boundaries are, in fact as a spiritual warrior and balanced individual it is better that others do not know exactly where those boundaries are because people like to test boundaries. Yes, childish, I know, but sadly that is where many people remain. The funny thing about boundaries though, they are flexible. How? Well if one creates the boundaries and does not seek external validation of those boundaries then they can be moved, bent, or even removed hence it actually makes the individual more flexible in controlling the outcome of any interaction between themselves and another.

When we broadcast our boundaries we are standing in our shadow ego and saying to the world this is me come and test me! When interacting with people who seem to broadcast their boundaries, or seek external validation, instead of falling into the trap of feeding their shadow here is a plan that works.

The best thing you can do is to validate their boundaries by acceptance and helping them to realize that they are safe with you, this then actually has the effect of giving them energy to move off that spot to become more of their own balanced individual;

IT:

- allows them to be more comfortable within their boundaries.

- aiding in rewiring that path and reinforcing the stronger more consensus driven conduit between their own shadow and their own non-shadow.

By behaving and being more balanced oneself, understanding and acting as the beacon and the safe harbor for another this is one of the true acts of a spiritual warrior. Do you always come out without scars? No, not every relationship can be saved. Some truly are toxic. However, applying these steps can help to stop a good relationship that is in trouble from becoming toxic.

9 COURAGE TO CHANGE

Obtaining courage is about acceptance and safety. There is a physiological response called the Fight or Flight response that is activated every time a person perceives an external threat. This response is hardwired into our being and is characterized by an increase in several chemicals in the body as well as other physiological changes with each threat. It is also called the "acute stress response" and was proposed by Walter Cannon in the 1920s as a function of most animals, including humans sympathetic nervous system.

It is considered a stress response caused by release of adrenaline and norepinephrine from the medulla of the adrenal glands. The release is triggered by a chemical in our sympathetic nerves. These chemicals facilitate increases in heart rate and breathing, constricting blood vessels and tightening muscles that activate this response.

There are 8 steps that one can utilize to assist with mitigating the fight or flight response.

1.   Recognize that Fight or Flight is a physiological response to an external perceived "threat"

2.   ACCEPT the physiological response

3.   Control the physiological response

4.   Examine the situation objectively and LISTEN to yourself – intuition

5.   Allow the situation to be viewed by you through your own filters

6.   Recognize that each situation is a new situation even when they are similar to past experiences

7.   Build a consensus within yourself for our true desire BEFORE ACTION

8.   DO the ACTION.

If an individual is aware and utilizes these techniques then they can have the courage to accept their own decisions, negating the fear aspects, and move forward in a positive, self-empowering way. Every person can develop what is necessary to be part of their chosen community. All it takes is first the internal dialog necessary to build the internal consensus and take the actions that one chooses to take. Then, walking that walk, others who share your commitment will come to you. They will find you, or you will find themIn order to understand what I mean by community, here are the traits of any community. They are safety, predictability, opportunities, access to goods and services, relationships between citizens, common values and goals, and a recognized place in the social structure.

Looking at courage to change and stand one's ground in the apparent chaos created when an individual chooses to step out with conviction into the world around them and change their shadow relationships.

As sentient beings, we are bombarded with information from a multiplicity of sources. We interpret it, analyze it, and act upon it. The courage to accept our own interpretation and the courage to act upon that interpretation is one of the key characteristics to this process. Many times an individual will perform the internal process and then choose not to act. This is the key, there are no victims. The individual is the only person who makes the decisions for themselves. The truth is that everyone makes these decisions. It is only the blame game, or the victim mentality that some use to give up the control of themselves and to utilize as an excuse for their own decisions.

Aristotle in section of Book III of Aristotle, *The Nicomachean Ethics*, defines courage as an individual who knows what they are doing, (knowledge), choose the action based on that knowledge, (wisdom), and do so from a fixed and permanent disposition (1105b33).

This means that one who is courageous face their greatest terrors. He is speaking of the battlefield where the dangers are "greatest and most glorious" (1115a30), and the most dangerous battlefield that the spiritual warrior faces is the one within themselves. Aristotle further reflects on the fact that City-states honor their dead since they choose the survival of the community by safeguarding the conditions for the common good. He goes on to say that there is viability choosing the courageous life for ITS own sake, not for anything external to it. He goes further to state that civic and moral or self-courage are similar, however the difference is that those who exhibit civic courage are looking for some kind of return for the courage and those who choose self-courage do so for their own happiness which is the true nature of his moral virtues, (1101a16), and which is pleasant in itself because virtuous actions are pleasant in themselves (1199a14).

In another place, Chapter 7 of the same work he talks on possibility of human happiness through the activity of contemplation; the "highest virtue" in us corresponding to the best in us (1177a12). Not only is this activity the most continuous, the most perfect and self-sufficient, one seeking no end beyond itself, but that which is most akin to the divine. The gods are the supremely happy beings, and we ought therefore to aim, not simply at living according to mortal thoughts, but instead, "so far as in us lies, to put on immortality" (1177b33).

Herein lies "the perfect happiness of man" (1177b33), not simply the secondary kind of "happiness" associated to the actions of the morally minded human.

To get a better understanding of this within context there is another concept that is central to Aristotle's work on courage. Ethics, as viewed by Aristotle, is an attempt to find out our chief end or highest good: an end which he maintains is final. He maintains that all of our aspirations must have an object or measure. This measure he calls happiness. This is something that all humans desire but seems illusive. For Aristotle happiness is based on human nature, and must begin from the facts of personal experience. It must then be found in the work and life which is unique to humans. This concept is central to all human existence and is to ensure happiness with one self. If we follow this logically then it follows therefore that true happiness lies in the active life of a rational being or in a perfect realization and outworking of the true soul and self, continued throughout a lifetime.

Aristotle expands his notion of happiness through an analysis of the human soul which structures and animates a living human organism. The parts of the soul which he divides into rational and irrational. It is the rational that has bearing on our discussion of courage. According to Aristotle, the Rational soul is part calculative and appetitive. The virtues he connects to the rational soul are

Intellectual and moral.

The part of ourselves which is responsible for our emotions and desires. It is truly in tune with what we have been discussing this entire book since humans have the distinct ability to control these desires with the help of reason. The human ability to properly control these desires is according to Aristotle, called moral virtue, and is the focus of morality. Aristotle notes that there is a purely rational part of the soul, the calculative, which is responsible for the human ability to contemplate, reason logically, and formulate scientific principles. The mastery of these abilities is called intellectual virtue. The courage to accept one's own decisions and to put them into action comes from the mastering of these two virtues.

Aristotle has several other points about the nature of moral virtues. First, he says this can be learned and is the outcome of both teaching and practice. Second, he notes that overthinking or regulating these desires either too much or too little, we create problems for ourselves. These problems can be seen as either jumping to conclusions or inactivity based on the need for further analysis.

According to this body of literature the way to regulate and to be able to function in balance is the concept of the mean. This is the core of Aristotle's account of moral virtue. A good example of this is say in response to fear develop courage. The key though is to develop this in balance to create a symbiotic relationship between these two aspects. The virtue of courage, then, lies at the mean between the excessive extreme of rashness, and the deficient extreme of cowardice, in his words it is "as a prudent man would determine it." Here is a good chart to help the spiritual warrior see the two components that work together for courage to accept.

I use his concepts of Deficiency   Mean and below

Deficiency	Mean	Excess
Cowardice	Courage	Rashness
Insensibility	Temperance	Intemperance
Illiberality	Liberality	Prodigality
Pettiness	Munificence	Vulgarity
Humble-mindedness	High-mindedness	Vaingloriness
Want of Ambition	Right Ambition	Over-ambition
Spiritlessness	Good Temper	Irascibility
Surliness	Friendly Civility	Obsequiousness
Ironical Depreciation	Sincerity	Boastfulness
Boorishness	Wittiness	Buffoonery
Shamelessness	Modesty	Bashfulness
Callousness	Resentment	Spitefulness

Each individual utilizes all these aspects in the way of the in order to create a balance within which to make decisions that are ultimately to the benefit of themselves.

Looking at the work of Carl Jung we see another way to look at courage. The word courage comes from the French root cour or coeur, which means heart. So courage has to do with the heart, that vital muscle that keeps our blood flowing and sustains life. Symbolically, the heart represents the spiritual core or innermost center of feelings, especially eros.

According to Stephen Diamond, PhD in an article called *What Is Courage? Lessons From the Cowardly Lion;*

Tapping into your inner hero. "Courage is required in almost every basic human activity or endeavor. For instance, to allow oneself to love and commit to another person takes immense courage. Separating from our parents and forging an independent life for ourselves is a courageous act. To survive an abusive, traumatic or neglected childhood with some sense of dignity and integrity intact demonstrates tremendous courage and resilience. Getting old demands courage. It takes courage to authentically be oneself in the world, and, as May (1976) points out in The Courage to Create, to dare to be truly creative, to artistically express and expose one's innermost self. Career or relationship changes require courage As does pursuing one's fondest dreams, or, as Joseph Campbell put it, to "follow your bliss." Indeed, it takes terrific courage to live, and to do so creatively, lovingly, meaningfully and productively."

This is one of the aspects of the hero archetype of C.J.Jung. The hero archetype is defined as: one who will get things done no matter what. They have the goal to gain mastery over themselves in a way that improves the world within and without. They do this by being as strong and competent as possible. A particular quote from his collected works volume 14, paragraph 752,

"Only one who has risked the fight with the dragon and is not overcome by it wins the "treasure hard to attain." He alone has a genuine claim to self-confidence, for he has faced the dark ground of his self and thereby has gained himself. This experience gives him faith and trust".

Here is another key, you are already a hero. You have faced the dragon within, reached accommodation and defeated its worst aspects and are ready to move forward with your decisions. It is a continuing conversation because each experience you receive is added to the hoard of the Jungian dragon, learning to share with your inner dragon is how you are able to have the courage to accept your own decisions.

This is showing us the chaos in that resides in our own mind. After all its hard to be happy for most individuals if they are in the middle of the whirlwind of chaos. The mind is a busy place There is something called Mind chatter. This is the endless, restless stream of incomplete thoughts, anxieties and self-talk which constantly pulses through our minds. In order to survive, our mind is always "on"—searching for possible threats, dangers, solutions and explanations. This is called our "strategic mind." The strategic mind is always "on"—scanning both our inner and outer world for possible threats to our well-being—either real or imagined. This constant vigilance of the mind not only distracts us with excessive worry but can also trigger the activation of our fight or flight response.

Sometimes, because of the mind's incessant chatter and worry, we even begin to anticipate dangers or threats that don't really exist. This is akin to a great acronym. Fear is **F**alse **E**xpectation **A**ppearing **R**eal.

Mark Twain said - "I've experienced many terrible things in my life, a few of which actually happened."

Underneath all the mind chatter and fight or flight anxiety lies a quiet place called our "inner voice", the "observer" or the "witness." The "inner voice" is what Walter Cannon, M.D., calls "the wisdom of the body." This quiet place allows us to move beyond our fears, beyond our anxieties and beyond our strategic mind—into a clearer understanding and knowing of what is true and loving. A quiet mind calms our overactive physiology, creating a sequence of physiologic and biochemical changes that improve our physical health.

OK so now we come to what may be uniquely human action which is looking toward the future. Do not propose to debate or even give an opinion on this concept, however, for sure, humans are capable of looking to the future. This is one of the things that is imperative when we make plans, or set goals. However, it also feeds into the switch that activates the fight or flight response.

Recognizing the physiological response to stress, helps the individual to understand and activate their tools in order to take back control from the aspect of survival. This is part of the feedback loop that one creates in order to build that inner consensus. It is also the way to assist us to obtain the courage to accept or own decisions.

The other thing this does is to help one to realize that – stress happens, and when they find themselves in a mode that is not part of their conscious choice that there is no judgment of themselves. Once this is accomplished then it is easier for the individual to build the consensus that is the key to good decisions and a balanced and harmonious life, or to defeat the dragon!

In order to consciously choose the attitudes and beliefs which are most empowering, we must learn to quiet our mind and quiet our body. By eliciting the relaxation response, we can stop the mind chatter, allowing us to move out of our strategic mind into the quiet mind, capable of conscious awareness and attention. The quiet mind opens up our perceptions and frees us to make the most positive choices regarding our lives. In this sense, the mind is likened to a pond of water. Restless thoughts are like pebbles thrown into the water. They send out a ripple of activity, disturbing the tranquil surface. When the water is constantly agitated with restless thoughts, we cannot see clearly to the bottom of the pond, which represents our inner wisdom. When we stop the restless thoughts, we calm the waters, enabling us to see clearly to the bottom—where our wisest, most enlightened self resides.

Once we have quieted ourselves from the internal chaos and made our decisions, stepped out in courage how do we deal with the ramifications from those outside ourselves? How do we remain happy with our decisions, even in the face of adversity and chaos from others? How do we deal with the disappointment that sometimes comes from those who we feel are closest?

The issue with happiness is that it is related to both our expectations and acceptance For example, if you go camping you expect that the weather will cooperate with you while you camp. If the weather turns and it rains, and gets a little cold you could rail against the weather, rail against the divine, become a victim, or, you could take it in stride. Now, some folk who camp prepare for the eventuality of inclement weather, and they camp on high ground, and when the weather begins to turn, they cover their campsite, tent, and some even have a canopy so that they can still enjoy the weather. They are what we call prepared. An individual who is prepared when interacting with the world also does not have agendas. I personally also do my best to not have expectations either. This does not mean that I say and feel that nothing will go right. That is something different. I accept, whatever happens based on my actions. My only expectation is what I personally can control and we already know that the only thing I can control is my actions, and how I respond to the actions of those around me.

Does this mean that I am never disappointed? Of course not, I get disappointed, how I handle that disappointment though is to accept the new circumstances exactly where they are and do not rail against anyone or anything. I do re-assess how that disappointment occurred and check to see if my expectations were unreasonable from the perspective of the other individuals involved. I also have conversation with the individuals in a reasonable, non-judgmental way, listening to what they say, and seeing if it was my expectation that was not correct. OR, to see if my expectation was unreasonable from the perspective of the others involved.

Now, I do get disappointed. And, I am sometimes blindsided by things that I do not expect. It is the action I choose to not re-act in a negative way to that disappointment. I always assess the situation from my own side and the side of the other and choose a new action. And I am happy with the result no matter what.

Each time one interacts with another it is from the place of total control and acceptance of their own and others actions. This is the key to happiness.

Do you have the courage to be happy no matter what?

Do you have the courage to be compassionate of everyone you come in contact with?

Do you have the courage to stand your ground?

Do you have the courage to accept others as you already accept yourself?

These are the questions to find real answers for in order to prevent you from creating Shadow Relationships.

BIBLIOGRAPHY

- Alderfer, C. (1972). *Existence, relatedness, & growth.* New York: Free Press.

- Allport, G. (1960). *Personality and social encounter: Selected essays.* New York: Beacon Press.

- Allport, G. (1961). *Pattern and growth in personality.* New York: Holt, Rinehart and Winston.

- Jens B. Asendorpf, Jens B. , Veronique Warkentin , Pierre-Marie Baudonniere *Self-Awareness and Other-Awareness II: Mirror Self-Recognition, Social Contingency Awareness, and Synchronic Imitation*

- Aristotle, *The Nicomachean Ethics, trans. W.D. Ross (1925)* Oxford, UK: Oxford University Press.

- Aubin, Ada and Rifkin, June The Complete Book of Astrology , St Martins Press, 1988

- Bly, Robert. *Iron John.* Decapo Press, 1984

- Cannon, Walter B. M.D. (1963) *Wisdom of the Body,* Norton Library

- Daniels, M. (2001). *Maslows's concept of self-actualization.* Retrieved February 2004, from http://www.mdani.demon.co.uk/archive/MDMaslow.htm

- Diamond, Stephen PhD (Apr 28, 2011) *What Is Courage? Lessons From the Cowardly Lion Tapping into your inner hero.*

- Franken, R. (2001). *Human motivation* (5th ed.).. Pacific Grove, CA: Brooks/Cole.

- Guest, Charlotte, (1812-1895), The Mabinogion, **Quaritch, 1877**

- Huitt, W. (2006, April 26). *Becoming a Brilliant Star: A framework for discussing formative holistic education.* Paper presented at the International Networking for Educational Transformation (iNet) Conference, Augusta, GA. Retrieved May 2006, from

  http://www.edpsycinteractive.org/brilstar/brilstar.html

- Huitt, W. (2007). *Success in the Conceptual Age: Another paradigm shift.* Paper delivered at the 32nd Annual Meeting of the Georgia Educational Research Association, Savannah, GA, October 26. Retrieved December 2007, fromhttp://chiron.valdosta.edu/whuitt/papers/conceptual_age_s.doc

- Institute for Management Excellence. (2001). The nine basic human needs. *Online Newsletter.* Retrieved February 2004, from http://www.itstime.com/print/jun97p.htm

- James, W. (1892/1962). *Psychology: Briefer course.* New York: Collier.

- Jung, CG (1875 – 1961) **Psychiatric Studies. The Collected Works of C. G. Jung** Vol. 1. 1953, ed. Michael Fordham, London: Routledge & Kegan Paul, and Princeton, N.J.: Bollingen.

- Jung, CG (1875 - 1961) *Answer to Job.* 1958 Princeton, N.J.: Princeton University Press

- Jung, CG (1875 - 1961) *The Development of Personality.* 1991 ed. London: Routledge. Collected Works Vol. 17

- Jung, CG (1875 – 1961) *The Undiscovered Self,* 2006 Signet

- Levy, Paul. *Tension of the Opposites.* (1999)

- Marshall, Johnathan *The Psychological Significance of Chaos and Disorder*, Canberra Jung Society Newsletter (Autumn 2011)

- Maslow, A. (1943). A theory of human motivation. *Psychological Review, 50,* 370-396. Retrieved June 2001, from http://psychclassics.yorku.ca/Maslow/motivation.htm.

- Maslow, A. (1954). *Motivation and personality.* New York: Harper.

- Maslow, A. (1971). *The farther reaches of human nature.* New York: The Viking Press.

- Maslow, A., & Lowery, R. (Ed.). (1998). *Toward a psychology of being* (3rd ed.). New York: Wiley & Sons.

- Mastin, Luke (2009) *Cosmological Theories throughout History. Retrieved May 2017,* from http://www.physicsoftheuniverse.com/cosmological.html.

- Mathes, E. (1981, Fall). Maslow's hierarchy of needs as a guide for living. *Journal of Humanistic Psychology, 21,* 69-72.

- Nohria, N , Lawrence, P., & Wilson, E. (2001). *Driven. How human nature shapes our choices.* San Francisco: Jossey-Bass.

- Norwood, G. (1999). Maslow's hierarchy of needs. *The Truth Vectors* (Part I). Retrieved May 2002, from http://www.deepermind.com/20maslow.htm

- Ryan, R., & Deci, E. (2000). Self-determination theory and the facilitation of intrinsic motivation, social development, and well-being. *American Psychologist, 55*(1), 68-78. Retrieved February 2004, fromhttp://www.psych.rochester.edu/SDT/publications/documents/2000RyanDeciSDT.pdf.

- Soper, B., Milford, G., & Rosenthal, G. (1995). Belief when evidence does not support theory. *Psychology & Marketing, 12*(5), 415-422.

- Thompson, M., Grace, C., & Cohen, L. (2001). *Best friends, worst enemies: Understanding the social lives of children.* New York: Ballantine Books. http://www.amazon.com/exec/obidos/ASIN/0345438094/qid=1024322725/sr=2-1/ref=sr_2_1/103-0382559-6049463

- Wahba, A., & Bridgewell, L. (1976). Maslow reconsidered: A review of research on the need hierarchy theory. *Organizational Behavior and Human Performance, 15*, 212-240.

- Waitley, D. (1996). *The new dynamics of goal setting: Flextactics for a fast-changing world.* New York: William Morrow.

- Willowhawk, Alfred *Manifesting True Desires: Learning from Arianrhod and the Tree of Life* (2013) Willowhawk Press

- Willoahwk, Alfred. *I Am Healer, Storyteller, and Warrior Priest: Learning from Arianrhod,* (2014) Willowhawk Press
- Woolfolk, Joanna Martin *The Only Astrology Book You'll Ever Need.* Taylor Trade Publications, 2006

ADDITIONAL
PUBLICATIONS

MANIFESTING TRUE DESIRES LEARNING FROM ARIANRHOD AND THE TREE OF LIFE

Publication Date: Jan 16 2013
     ISBN/EAN13:1481963635 / 9781481963633
     Page Count: 134
     Binding Type: US Trade Paper
     Trim Size: 6" x 9"
     Language: English
     Related Categories: Religion / Mysticism

Have you ever wondered why you don't get the things you desire in life? Have you ever considered that the answer to this question lies in how you asked for the blessing? Do you truly believe you have control over your own destiny? Manifesting True Desires: Learning from Arianrhod and the Tree of Life combines ancient Welsh Traditional learning with a deep understanding of the Kabbalah and together, is a system designed to answer these questions and more, putting the true power of manifestation in your hands.

This book has been brought forward to teach a whole new way to work with your own powers of manifestation in everyday life and to assist you in obtaining your own truest desires.

I AM HEALER STORYTELLER AND WARRIOR PRIEST: LEARNING FROM ARIANRHOD

PUBLICATION DATE: JUN 17 2015
ISBN/EAN13:1507817088 / 9781507817087
PAGE COUNT: 234
BINDING TYPE: US TRADE PAPER
TRIM SIZE: 6" X 9"
LANGUAGE: ENGLISH
RELATED CATEGORIES: RELIGION / PAGANISM & NEO-PAGANISM

ARIANRHOD OFT TIMES MISUNDERSTOOD AND ELUSIVE IS HERE ILLUMINATED FROM ANCIENT MANUSCRIPTS AND LEGENDS. HER STORY IS ONE OF DANGER, BETRAYAL AND EMBARRASSMENT. SHE RAISED ABOVE ALL THAT TO BECOME A POWERFUL FORCE IN THE ANCIENT WORLD HONORED BY MANY. THIS WORK SHARES HER STORY AND HOW SHE ASSISTS US IN BECOMING THE HEALER, STORYTELLER, AND WARRIOR PRIEST(ESS).

HAWK SIGHTINGS

Publication Date: Dec 25 2012
ISBN/EAN13:0615183387 / 9780615183381
Page Count:60
Binding Type:US Trade Paper
Trim Size:6" x 9"
Language:English
Related Categories:Poetry / Subjects & Themes / Love

Shamanic Poetry Collection. Designed to assist you in connecting to your Inner Shaman 25 poems each full of amazing imagry to tap your Shamanic Soul
These poems are illustrated by reknown artist Ziza - (Will O' Wellspring)

CREATING GUIDED MEDITATIONS FOR YOURSELF AND OTHERS

ISBN/EAN13:1544011717 / 9781544011714
Page Count:80
Binding Type:US Trade Paper
Trim Size:5" x 8"
Language:English
Related Categories:Body, Mind & Spirit / Mindfulness & Meditation

Sometimes we are deaf when it comes to hearing the messages of the divine. However one of the best tools to hear these messages, as well as tap into our higher selves is guided meditations.
A really good guided meditation will assist an individual to really hear what is going on in his or her unconscious, also known as the universal consciousness or the divine.
This book teaches you an easy and safe method to create guided meditations, which you can then use to help yourself in many aspects of your life. For those who work as counselors, teachers, or healers, this book addresses the ethics involved in creating meditations for others, as well as how best to serve your clients.

MEDITATIONS FOR LIFE

This CD has 4 16 minute guided Meditations by me for your spiritual pleasure.

They are designed to enhance your connection to your own spiritual path Each meditation works on one aspect of spiritual health

It Includes:

Connecting with the Universal Consciousness
A guided meditation to lead you to meet and speak with the Divine as YOU define it!

The Healing Pool
Go to this fantastic Spiritual and Physical Healing Pool of Celtic Myth and start healing YOURSELF

The Cabin
Everyone needs some time alone! Even if you are a people person! The Cabin in a soft rain is just
the place!

The Faire
Go to a Old Fashion Celtic Market Faire! Meet the bards, dance, eat, sleep and have FUN!

THE WARRIOR WITHIN RELEASE

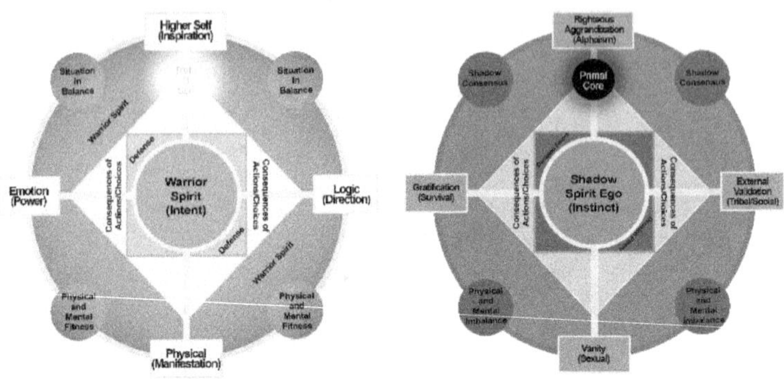

The concept of the Warrior is in every culture. No matter what your spiritual path, there is a Warrior.

Learn to associate, and speak to your own Warrior Spirit. We will learn how to recognize the **four bodies** and their integration with the physical and mental selves to become a whole person. This is **personal and specific to YOU.** You will draw upon your personal symbols and protectors to bring this rich and beautiful heritage to life. So, **welcome to your changed life.**

Fully tap into the Shadow and Non-Shadow Warrior in this intensive program.

ABOUT THE AUTHOR

Alfred Willowhawk, DMsc, DD is a 20 year veteran of spiritual counseling, coaching and training. He is ordained as a metaphysical minister by the University of Metaphysics with a Doctorate of Metaphysical Science. He is one of the founders and senior clergy of the Wite Rayvn Metaphysical Church . He has been helping people manifest themselves to their highest potential for over 20 years. He has also a Reki Master, and creator of the healing system Celtic Transformational Healing and a co-founder of the Wite Rayvn Metaphysical Church. His work with men and women to embrace the Warrior of Spirit within has assisted many people over the last 10 years. He is an MKP brother and has facilitated the initiation of men and women into the Warrior of Spirit. Alfred is the host of the weekly radio show The Warrior Within Show on WCAS radio Friday nights at 9 PM Eastern.